OMEROS

Derek Walcott was born in St Lucia in 1930. He was educated at St Mary's College and the University of the West Indies. He has taught at the universities of Columbia, Yale and Harvard. Currently, he is Professor of English at Boston University, where he teaches writing courses in poetry and drama. Among his many plays are *Dream on Monkey Mountain* (for which he won an off-Broadway award), *Pantomime* and *Pi-jean and his Brothers*. His *Collected Poems 1948–1984* was published in 1986 and *The Arkansas Testament* in 1987. He was awarded the Queen's Medal for poetry in 1988.

Derek Walcott divides his time between Boston and the Caribbean.

OMEROS
Derek Walcott

faber and faber
LONDON · BOSTON

First published in the USA in 1990
by Farrar, Straus and Giroux, Inc., New York
and simultaneously in Canada
by Collins Publishers, Toronto
First published in Great Britain in 1990
by Faber and Faber Limited
3 Queen Square London WC1N 3AU

Printed in England by Clays Ltd, St Ives plc

A CIP record of this book
is available from the British Library

ISBN 0-571-14459-4

6 8 10 9 7 5

ENL
R535/9K

FOR MY SHIPMATES IN THIS CRAFT,

FOR MY BROTHER, RODERICK,

& FOR ROGER STRAUS

OMEROS

BOOK ONE

Chapter I

I

"This is how, one sunrise, we cut down them canoes."
Philoctete smiles for the tourists, who try taking
his soul with their cameras. "Once wind bring the news

to the *laurier-cannelles*, their leaves start shaking
the minute the axe of sunlight hit the cedars,
because they could see the axes in our own eyes.

Wind lift the ferns. They sound like the sea that feed us
fishermen all our life, and the ferns nodded 'Yes,
the trees have to die.' So, fists jam in our jacket,

cause the heights was cold and our breath making feathers
like the mist, we pass the rum. When it came back, it
give us the spirit to turn into murderers.

I lift up the axe and pray for strength in my hands
to wound the first cedar. Dew was filling my eyes,
but I fire one more white rum. Then we advance."

For some extra silver, under a sea-almond,
he shows them a scar made by a rusted anchor,
rolling one trouser-leg up with the rising moan

of a conch. It has puckered like the corolla
of a sea-urchin. He does not explain its cure.
"It have some things"—he smiles—"worth more than a dollar."

He has left it to a garrulous waterfall
to pour out his secret down La Sorcière, since
the tall laurels fell, for the ground-dove's mating call

to pass on its note to the blue, tacit mountains
whose talkative brooks, carrying it to the sea,
turn into idle pools where the clear minnows shoot

and an egret stalks the reeds with one rusted cry
as it stabs and stabs the mud with one lifting foot.
Then silence is sawn in half by a dragonfly

as eels sign their names along the clear bottom-sand,
when the sunrise brightens the river's memory
and waves of huge ferns are nodding to the sea's sound.

Although smoke forgets the earth from which it ascends,
and nettles guard the holes where the laurels were killed,
an iguana hears the axes, clouding each lens

over its lost name, when the hunched island was called
"Iounalao," "Where the iguana is found."
But, taking its own time, the iguana will scale

the rigging of vines in a year, its dewlap fanned,
its elbows akimbo, its deliberate tail
moving with the island. The slit pods of its eyes

ripened in a pause that lasted for centuries,
that rose with the Aruacs' smoke till a new race
unknown to the lizard stood measuring the trees.

These were their pillars that fell, leaving a blue space
for a single God where the old gods stood before.
The first god was a gommier. The generator

began with a whine, and a shark, with sidewise jaw,
sent the chips flying like mackerel over water
into trembling weeds. Now they cut off the saw,

still hot and shaking, to examine the wound it
had made. They scraped off its gangrenous moss, then ripped
the wound clear of the net of vines that still bound it

to this earth, and nodded. The generator whipped
back to its work, and the chips flew much faster as
the shark's teeth gnawed evenly. They covered their eyes

from the splintering nest. Now, over the pastures
of bananas, the island lifted its horns. Sunrise
trickled down its valleys, blood splashed on the cedars,

and the grove flooded with the light of sacrifice.
A gommier was cracking. Its leaves an enormous
tarpaulin with the ridgepole gone. The creaking sound

made the fishermen leap back as the angling mast
leant slowly towards the troughs of ferns; then the ground
shuddered under the feet in waves, then the waves passed.

Achille looked up at the hole the laurel had left.
He saw the hole silently healing with the foam
of a cloud like a breaker. Then he saw the swift

crossing the cloud-surf, a small thing, far from its home,
confused by the waves of blue hills. A thorn vine gripped
his heel. He tugged it free. Around him, other ships

were shaping from the saw. With his cutlass he made
a swift sign of the cross, his thumb touching his lips
while the height rang with axes. He swayed back the blade,

and hacked the limbs from the dead god, knot after knot,
wrenching the severed veins from the trunk as he prayed:
"Tree! You can be a canoe! Or else you cannot!"

The bearded elders endured the decimation
of their tribe without uttering a syllable
of that language they had uttered as one nation,

the speech taught their saplings: from the towering babble
of the cedar to green vowels of *bois-campêche*.
The *bois-flot* held its tongue with the *laurier-cannelle*,

the red-skinned logwood endured the thorns in its flesh,
while the Aruacs' patois crackled in the smell
of a resinous bonfire that turned the leaves brown

with curling tongues, then ash, and their language was lost.
Like barbarians striding columns they have brought down,
the fishermen shouted. The gods were down at last.

Like pygmies they hacked the trunks of wrinkled giants
for paddles and oars. They were working with the same
concentration as an army of fire-ants.

But vexed by the smoke for defaming their forest,
blow-darts of mosquitoes kept needling Achille's trunk.
He frotted white rum on both forearms that, at least,

those that he flattened to asterisks would die drunk.
They went for his eyes. They circled them with attacks
that made him weep blindly. Then the host retreated

to high bamboo like the archers of Aruacs
running from the muskets of cracking logs, routed
by the fire's banner and the remorseless axe

hacking the branches. The men bound the big logs first
with new hemp and, like ants, trundled them to a cliff
to plunge through tall nettles. The logs gathered that thirst

for the sea which their own vined bodies were born with.
Now the trunks in eagerness to become canoes
ploughed into breakers of bushes, making raw holes

of boulders, feeling not death inside them, but use—
to roof the sea, to be hulls. Then, on the beach, coals
were set in their hollows that were chipped with an adze.

A flat-bed truck had carried their rope-bound bodies.
The charcoals, smouldering, cored the dugouts for days
till heat widened the wood enough for ribbed gunwales.

Under his tapping chisel Achille felt their hollows
exhaling to touch the sea, lunging towards the haze
of bird-printed islets, the beaks of their parted bows.

Then everything fit. The pirogues crouched on the sand
like hounds with sprigs in their teeth. The priest
sprinkled them with a bell, then he made the swift's sign.

When he smiled at Achille's canoe, *In God We Troust*,
Achille said: "Leave it! Is God' spelling and mine."
After Mass one sunrise the canoes entered the troughs

of the surpliced shallows, and their nodding prows
agreed with the waves to forget their lives as trees;
one would serve Hector and another, Achilles.

III

Achille peed in the dark, then bolted the half-door shut.
It was rusted from sea-blast. He hoisted the fishpot
with the crab of one hand; in the hole under the hut

he hid the cinder-block step. As he neared the depot,
the dawn breeze salted him coming up the grey street
past sleep-tight houses, under the sodium bars

of street-lamps, to the dry asphalt scraped by his feet;
he counted the small blue sparks of separate stars.
Banana fronds nodded to the undulating

anger of roosters, their cries screeching like red chalk
drawing hills on a board. Like his teacher, waiting,
the surf kept chafing at his deliberate walk.

By the time they met at the wall of the concrete shed
the morning star had stepped back, hating the odour
of nets and fish-guts; the light was hard overhead

and there was a horizon. He put the net by the door
of the depot, then washed his hands in its basin.
The surf did not raise its voice, even the ribbed hounds

around the canoes were quiet; a flask of l'absinthe
was passed by the fishermen, who made smacking sounds
and shook at the bitter bark from which it was brewed.

This was the light that Achille was happiest in.
When, before their hands gripped the gunwales, they stood
for the sea-width to enter them, feeling their day begin.

Chapter II

I

Hector was there. Theophile also. In this light,
they have only Christian names. Placide, Pancreas,
Chrysostom, Maljo, Philoctete with his head white

as the coiled surf. They shipped the lances of oars,
placed them parallel in the grave of the gunwales
like man and wife. They scooped the leaf-bilge from the planks,

loosened knots from the bodies of flour-sack sails,
while Hector, at the shallows' edge, gave a quick thanks,
with the sea for a font, before he waded, thigh-in.

The rest walked up the sand with identical stride
except for foam-haired Philoctete. The sore on his shin
still unhealed, like a radiant anemone. It had come

from a scraping, rusted anchor. The pronged iron
peeled the skin in a backwash. He bent to the foam,
sprinkling it with a salt hiss. Soon he would run,

hobbling, to the useless shade of an almond,
with locked teeth, then wave them off from the shame
of his smell, and once more they would leave him alone

under its leoparding light. This sunrise the same
damned business was happening. He felt the sore twitch
its wires up to his groin. With his hop-and-drop

limp, hand clutching one knee, he left the printed beach
to crawl up the early street to Ma Kilman's shop.
She would open and put the white rum within reach.

His shipmates watched him, then they hooked hands like anchors
under the hulls, rocking them; the keels sheared dry sand
till the wet sand resisted, rattling the oars

that lay parallel amidships; then, to the one sound
of curses and prayers at the logs jammed as a wedge,
one after one, as their tins began to rattle,

the pirogues slid to the shallows' nibbling edge,
towards the encouraging sea. The loose logs swirled
in surf, face down, like warriors from a battle

lost somewhere on the other shore of the world.
They were dragged to a place under the manchineels
to lie there face upward, the sun moving over their brows

with the stare of myrmidons hauled up by the heels
high up from the tide-mark where the pale crab burrows.
The fishermen brushed their palms. Now all the canoes

were riding the pink morning swell. They drew their bows
gently, the way grooms handle horses in the sunrise,
flicking the ropes like reins, pinned them by the nose—

Praise Him, Morning Star, St. Lucia, Light of My Eyes,
threw bailing tins in them, and folded their bodies across
the tilting hulls, then sculled one oar in the slack

of the stern. Hector rattled out his bound canvas
to gain ground with the gulls, hoping to come back
before that conch-coloured dusk low pelicans cross.

I I

Seven Seas rose in the half-dark to make coffee.
Sunrise was heating the ring of the horizon
and clouds were rising like loaves. By the heat of the

glowing iron rose he slid the saucepan's base on-
to the ring and anchored it there. The saucepan shook
from the weight of water in it, then it settled.

His kettle leaked. He groped for the tin chair and took
his place near the saucepan to hear when it bubbled.
It would boil but not scream like a bosun's whistle

to let him know it was ready. He heard the dog's
morning whine under the boards of the house, its tail
thudding to be let in, but he envied the pirogues

already miles out at sea. Then he heard the first breeze
washing the sea-almond's wares; last night there had been
a full moon white as his plate. He saw with his ears.

He warmed with the roofs as the sun began to climb.
Since the disease had obliterated vision,
when the sunset shook the sea's hand for the last time—

and an inward darkness grew where the moon and sun
indistinctly altered—he moved by a sixth sense,
like the moon without an hour or second hand,

wiped clean as the plate that he now began to rinse
while the saucepan bubbled; blindness was not the end.
It was not a palm-tree's dial on the noon sand.

He could feel the sunlight creeping over his wrists.
The sunlight moved like a cat along the palings
of a sandy street; he felt it unclench the fists

of the breadfruit tree in his yard, run the railings
of the short iron bridge like a harp, its racing
stick rippling with the river; he saw the lagoon

behind the church, and in it, stuck like a basin,
the rusting enamel image of the full moon.
He lowered the ring to sunset under the pan.

The dog scratched at the kitchen door for him to open
but he made it wait. He drummed the kitchen table
with his fingers. Two blackbirds quarrelled at breakfast.

Except for one hand he sat as still as marble,
with his egg-white eyes, fingers recounting the past
of another sea, measured by the stroking oars.

O open this day with the conch's moan, Omeros,
as you did in my boyhood, when I was a noun
gently exhaled from the palate of the sunrise.

A lizard on the sea-wall darted its question
at the waking sea, and a net of golden moss
brightened the reef, which the sails of their far canoes

avoided. Only in you, across centuries
of the sea's parchment atlas, can I catch the noise
of the surf lines wandering like the shambling fleece

of the lighthouse's flock, that Cyclops whose blind eye
shut from the sunlight. Then the canoes were galleys
over which a frigate sawed its scythed wings slowly.

In you the seeds of grey almonds guessed a tree's shape,
and the grape leaves rusted like serrated islands,
and the blind lighthouse, sensing the edge of a cape,

paused like a giant, a marble cloud in its hands,
to hurl its boulder that splashed into phosphorous
stars; then a black fisherman, his stubbled chin coarse

as a dry sea-urchin's, hoisted his flour-sack
sail on its bamboo spar, and scanned the opening line
of our epic horizon; now I can look back

to rocks that see their own feet when light nets the waves,
as the dugouts set out with ebony captains,
since it was your light that startled our sunlit wharves

where schooners swayed idly, moored to their cold capstans.
A wind turns the harbour's pages back to the voice
that hummed in the vase of a girl's throat: "Omeros."

"O-meros," she laughed. "That's what we call him in Greek,"
stroking the small bust with its boxer's broken nose,
and I thought of Seven Seas sitting near the reek

of drying fishnets, listening to the shallows' noise.
I said: "Homer and Virg are New England farmers,
and the winged horse guards their gas-station, you're right."

I felt the foam head watching as I stroked an arm, as
cold as its marble, then the shoulders in winter light
in the studio attic. I said, "Omeros,"

and O was the conch-shell's invocation, *mer* was
both mother and sea in our Antillean patois,
os, a grey bone, and the white surf as it crashes

and spreads its sibilant collar on a lace shore.
Omeros was the crunch of dry leaves, and the washes
that echoed from a cave-mouth when the tide has ebbed.

The name stayed in my mouth. I saw how light was webbed
on her Asian cheeks, defined her eyes with a black
almond's outline, as Antigone turned and said:

"I'm tired of America, it's time for me to go back
to Greece. I miss my islands." I write, it returns—
the way she turned and shook out the black gust of hair.

I saw how the surf printed its lace in patterns
on the shore of her neck, then the lowering shallows
of silk swirled at her ankles, like surf without noise,

and felt that another cold bust, not hers, but yours
saw this with stone almonds for eyes, its broken nose
turning away, as the rustling silk agrees.

But if it could read between the lines of her floor
like a white-hot deck uncaulked by Antillean heat,
to the shadows in its hold, its nostrils might flare

at the stench from manacled ankles, the coffled feet
scraping like leaves, and perhaps the inculpable marble
would have turned its white seeds away, to widen

the bow of its mouth at the horror under her table,
from the lyre of her armchair draped with its white chiton,
to do what the past always does: suffer, and stare.

She lay calm as a port, and a cloud covered her
with my shadow; then a prow with painted eyes
slowly emerged from the fragrant rain of black hair.

And I heard a hollow moan exhaled from a vase,
not for kings floundering in lances of rain; the prose
of abrupt fishermen cursing over canoes.

Chapter III

I

"*Touchez-i, encore: N'ai fendre choux-ous-ou, salope!*"
"Touch it again, and I'll split your arse, you bitch!"
"*Moi j'a dire—'ous pas prêter un rien. 'Ous ni shallope,*

'ous ni seine, 'ous croire 'ous ni choeur campêche?"
"I told you, borrow nothing of mine. You have a canoe,
and a net. Who you think you are? Logwood Heart?"

" *'Ous croire 'ous c'est roi Gros Îlet? Voleur bomme!"*
"You think you're king of Gros Îlet, you tin-stealer?"
Then in English: "I go show you who is king! Come!"

Hector came out from the shade. And Achille, the
moment he saw him carrying the cutlass, *un homme
fou*, a madman eaten with envy, replaced the tin

he had borrowed from Hector's canoe neatly back in the prow
of Hector's boat. Then Achille, who had had enough
of this madman, wiped and hefted his own blade.

And now the villagers emerged from the green shade
of the almonds and wax-leaved manchineels, for the face-off
that Hector wanted. Achille walked off and waited

at the warm shallows' edge. Hector strode towards him.
The villagers followed, as the surf abated
its sound, its fear cowering at the beach's rim.

Then, far out at sea, in a sparkling shower
arrows of rain arched from the emerald breakwater
of the reef, the shafts travelling with clear power

in the sun, and behind them, ranged for the slaughter,
stood villagers, shouting, with a sound like the shoal,
and hoisting arms to the light. Hector ran, splashing

in shallows mixed with the drizzle, towards Achille,
his cutlass lifted. The surf, in anger, gnashing
its tail like a foaming dogfight. Men can kill

their own brothers in rage, but the madman who tore
Achille's undershirt from one shoulder also tore
at his heart. The rage that he felt against Hector

was shame. To go crazy for an old bailing tin
crusted with rust! The duel of these fishermen
was over a shadow and its name was Helen.

I I

Ma Kilman had the oldest bar in the village.
Its gingerbread balcony had mustard gables
with green trim round the eaves, the paint wrinkled with age.

In the cabaret downstairs there were wooden tables
for the downslap of dominoes. A bead curtain
tinkled every time she came through it. A neon

sign endorsed Coca-Cola under the NO PAIN
CAFÉ ALL WELCOME. The NO PAIN was not her own
idea, but her dead husband's. "Is a prophecy,"

Ma Kilman would laugh. A hot street led to the beach
past the small shops and the clubs and a pharmacy
in whose angling shade, his khaki dog on a leash,

the blind man sat on his crate after the pirogues
set out, muttering the dark language of the blind,
gnarled hands on his stick, his ears as sharp as the dog's.

Sometimes he would sing and the scraps blew on the wind
when her beads rubbed their rosary. Old St. Omere.
He claimed he'd sailed round the world. "Monsieur Seven Seas"

1 7

they christened him, from a cod-liver-oil label
with its wriggling swordfish. But his words were not clear.
They were Greek to her. Or old African babble.

Across wires of hot asphalt the blind singer
seemed to be numbering things. Who knows if his eyes
saw through the shades, tapping his cane with one finger?

She helped him draw his veteran's compensation
every first of the month from the small Post Office.
He never complained about his situation

like the rest of them. The corner box, and the heat
on his hands would make him shift his box to the shade.
Ma Kilman saw Philoctete hobbling up the street,

so she rose from her corner window, and she laid
out the usual medicine for him, a flask of white
acajou, and a jar of yellow Vaseline,

a small enamel basin of ice. He would wait
in the No Pain Café all day. There he would lean
down and anoint the mouth of the sore on his shin.

I I I

"Mais qui ça qui rivait-'ous, Philoctete?"
                                         "Moin blessé."
"But what is wrong wif you, Philoctete?"
                                         "I am blest
wif this wound, Ma Kilman, *qui pas ka guérir pièce.*

18

Which will never heal."
                              "Well, you must take it easy.
Go home and lie down, give the foot a lickle rest."
Philoctete, his trouser-legs rolled, stares out to sea

from the worn rumshop window. The itch in the sore
tingles like the tendrils of the anemone,
and the puffed blister of Portuguese man-o'-war.

He believed the swelling came from the chained ankles
of his grandfathers. Or else why was there no cure?
That the cross he carried was not only the anchor's

but that of his race, for a village black and poor
as the pigs that rooted in its burning garbage,
then were hooked on the anchors of the abattoir.

Ma Kilman was sewing. She looked up and saw his face
squinting from the white of the street. He was waiting
to pass out on the table. This went on for days.

The ice turned to warm water near the self-hating
gesture of clenching his head tight in both hands. She
heard the boys in blue uniforms, going to school,

screaming at his elbow: "Pheeloh! Pheelosophee!"
A mummy embalmed in Vaseline and alcohol.
In the Egyptian silence she muttered softly:

"It have a flower somewhere, a medicine, and ways
my grandmother would boil it. I used to watch ants
climbing her white flower-pot. But, God, in which place?"

Where was this root? What senna, what tepid tisanes,
could clean the branched river of his corrupted blood,
whose sap was a wounded cedar's? What did it mean,

this name that felt like a fever? Well, one good heft
of his garden-cutlass would slice the damned name clean
from its rotting yam. He said, *"Merci."* Then he left.

Chapter IV

I

North of the village is a logwood grove whose thorns
litter its dry shade. The broken road has boulders,
and quartz that glistens like rain. The logwoods were once

part of an estate with its windmill as old as
the village below it. The abandoned road runs
past huge rusted cauldrons, vats for boiling the sugar,

and blackened pillars. These are the only ruins
left here by history, if history is what they are.
The twisted logwood trunks are orange from sea-blast;

above them is a stand of surprising cactus.
Philoctete limped to his yam garden there. He passed
through the estate shuddering, cradling his cutlass,

bayed at by brown, knotted sheep repeating his name.
"Beeeeeh, Philoctete!" Here, in the Atlantic wind,
the almonds bent evenly like a candle-flame.

The thought of candles brought his own death to mind.
The wind turned the yam leaves like maps of Africa,
their veins bled white, as Philoctete, hobbling, went

between the yam beds like a patient growing weaker
down a hospital ward. His skin was a nettle,
his head a market of ants; he heard the crabs groan

from arthritic pincers, he felt a mole-cricket drill
his sore to the bone. His knee was radiant iron,
his chest was a sack of ice, and behind the bars

of his rusted teeth, like a mongoose in a cage,
a scream was mad to come out; his tongue tickled its claws
on the roof of his mouth, rattling its bars in rage.

He saw the blue smoke from the yards, the bamboo poles
weighed down by nets, the floating feather of the priest.
When cutlass cut smoke, when cocks surprise their arseholes

by shitting eggs, he cursed, *black people go get rest*
from God; at which point a fierce cluster of arrows
targeted the sore, and he screamed in the yam rows.

He stretched out the foot. He edged the razor-sharp steel
through pleading finger and thumb. The yam leaves recoiled
in a cold sweat. He hacked every root at the heel.

He hacked them at the heel, noticing how they curled,
head-down without their roots. He cursed the yams:
                                                    "Salope!
You all see what it's like without roots in this world?"

Then sobbed, his face down in the slaughtered leaves. A sap
trickled from their gaping stems like his own sorrow.
A fly quickly washed its hands of the massacre.

Philoctete felt an ant crawling across his brow.
It was the breeze. He looked up at a blue acre
and a branch where a swift settled without a cry.

He felt the village through his back, heard the sea-hum
of transports below. The sea-swift was watching him.
Then it twittered seaward, swallowed in the cloud-foam.

For as long as it takes a single drop to dry
on the wax of a dasheen leaf, Philoctete lay
on his pebbled spine on hot earth watching the sky

altering white continents with its geography.
He would ask God's pardon. Over the quiet bay
the grass smelt good and the clouds changed beautifully.

Next he heard warriors rushing towards battle,
but it was wind lifting the dead yams, the rattle
of a palm's shaken spears. Herdsmen haieing cattle

who set out to found no cities; they were the found,
who were bound for no victories; they were the bound,
who levelled nothing before them; they were the ground.

He would be the soul of patience, like an old horse
stamping one hoof in a pasture, rattling its mane
or swishing its tail as flies keep circling its sores;

if a horse could endure afflictions so could men.
He held to a branch and tested his dead hoof once
on the springy earth. It felt weightless as a sponge.

I sat on the white terrace waiting for the cheque.
Our waiter, in a black bow-tie, plunged through the sand
between the full deck-chairs, bouncing to discotheque

music from the speakers, a tray sailed in one hand.
The tourists revolved, grilling their backs in their noon
barbecue. The waiter was having a hard time

with his leather soles. They kept sliding down a dune,
but his tray teetered without spilling gin-and-lime
on a scorched back. He was determined to meet the

beach's demands, like a Lawrence of St. Lucia,
except that he was trudging towards a litre
of self-conscious champagne. Like any born loser

he soon kicked the bucket. He rested his tray down,
wiped the sand from the ice-cubes, then plunked the cubes in
the bucket, then the bottle; after this was done,

he seemed ready to help the wife stuff her boobs in
her halter, while her husband sat boiling with rage
like a towelled sheik. Then Lawrence frowned at a mirage.

That was when I turned with him towards the village,
and saw, through the caging wires of the noon sky,
a beach with its padding panther; now the mirage

dissolved to a woman with a madras head-tie,
but the head proud, although it was looking for work.
I felt like standing in homage to a beauty

that left, like a ship, widening eyes in its wake.
"Who the hell is that?" a tourist near my table
asked a waitress. The waitress said, "She? She too proud!"

As the carved lids of the unimaginable
ebony mask unwrapped from its cotton-wool cloud,
the waitress sneered, "Helen." And all the rest followed.

Chapter V

I

Major Plunkett gently settled his Guinness, wiped
the rime of gold foam freckling his pensioned moustache
with a surf-curling tongue. Adjacently, Maud sipped

quietly, wifely, an ale. Under the peaked thatch
designed like a kraal facing the weathered village,
the raffia decor was empty. He heard the squeak

of Maud's weight when she shifted. The usual mirage
of clouds in full canvas steered towards Martinique.
This was their watering-hole, this rigid custom

of lowering the yardarm from the same raffia chairs
once a week at one, between the bank and the farm,
once Maud delivered her orchids, for all these years

of self-examining silence. Maud stirred the ends
of damp curls from her nape. The Major drummed the edge
of the bar and twirled a straw coaster. Their silence

was a mutual communion. They'd been out here
since the war and his wound. Pigs. Orchids. Their marriage
a silver anniversary of bright water

that glittered like Glen-da-Lough in Maud's home county
of Wicklow, but for Dennis, in his khaki shirt
and capacious shorts in which he'd served with Monty,

the crusted tourists were corpses in the desert
from the Afrika Korps. *Pro Rommel, pro mori.*
The regimental brandies stiffened on the shelves

near Napoleonic cognacs. All history
in a dusty Beefeater's gin. We helped ourselves
to these green islands like olives from a saucer,

munched on the pith, then spat their sucked stones on a plate,
like a melon's black seeds. *Pro honoris causa,*
but in whose honour did his head-wound graduate?

This was their Saturday place, not a corner-pub,
not the wrought-iron Victoria. He had resigned
from that haunt of middle-clarse farts, an old club

with more pompous arses than any flea could find,
a replica of the Raj, with gins-and-tonic
from black, white-jacketed servitors whose sonic

judgement couldn't distinguish a secondhand-car
salesman from Manchester from the phony pukka
tones of ex-patriates. He was no officer,

but he'd found himself saying things like "Luverly,"
"Right-o," and, Jesus Christ, "Ta!" from a wicker chair,
with the other farts exchanging their brusque volley

in the class war. Every one of them a liar
dyeing his roots, their irrepressible Cockney,
overdoing impatience. Clods from Lancashire

surprised by servants, outpricing their own value
and their red-kneed wives with accents like cutlery
spilled from a drawer. For them, the fields of his valour,

the war in the desert under Montgomery,
and the lilac flowers under the crosses were
preserved by being pickled at the Victoria.

He'd played the officer's pitch. Though he felt ashamed,
it paid off. The sand grit in his throat, the Rover,
all that sort of stuff. The khaki shorts that proclaimed

his forgotten service. Well, all that was over,
but not the class war that denigrated the dead
face down in the sand, beyond Alexandria.

The flags pinned to a map. The prone crosses
of tourists sprawled out far from the red lifeguard's flag,
like those of his comrades with sand seaming their eyes.

What was it all for? A bagpipe's screech and a rag.
Well, why not? In war, the glory was the yeoman's;
the kids from drizzling streets; they fell like those Yanks

in a sun twice as fierce, Tobruk and Alamein's,
their corpses black in the shade of the shattered tanks,
their bodies dragged like towels to a palm-tree's shade.

Those lines of white surf raced like the applauding streets
alongside the Eighth Army when Montgomery broke
the back of the Afrika Korps. Blokes in white sheets

flinging caps like spray as we piped into Tobruk
and I leant on the tank turret while bagpipes screeched
ahead of those grinning Tommies. I wept with pride.

Tears prickled his eyes. Maud reached across the saucer
and gripped his fingers. He knew she could see inside
the wound in his head. His white nurse. His officer.

I I

Not club-mates. Chums, companions. Comrades-in-arms.
They crouched, hands on helmets, while the Messerschmitt's gun
stitched, in staccato succession, miniature palms

along the top of the trench. He shot up. Again
Tumbly pulled him down. "Just keep yer bleedin' 'ead low!"
Scott was running to them, laughing, but the only thing

funny about him was the fact that one elbow
didn't have the rest of the arm. He jerked the thing
from the stump, mimicking a Kraut salute; then, as

his astonishment passed, he sagged down from the knees
with that grin. And I turned to Tumbly and his eyes
were open but not moving; then an awful noise

lifted all of us up from the sand and I guess
I was hit then, but I could remember nothing
for months, in casualty. Oh yes! that business

of Tumbly's eyes. The sky in them. Scottie laughing.
Tell them that at the Victoria, in the noise
of ice-cubes tinkling and the draft-beer frothing.

This wound I have stitched into Plunkett's character.
He has to be wounded, affliction is one theme
of this work, this fiction, since every "I" is a

fiction finally. Phantom narrator, resume:
Tumbly. Blue holes for his eyes. And Scottie wiser
when the shock passed. Plain men. Not striking. Not handsome.

Through the Moorish arches of the hospital ward,
with a cloud wrapped around his head like an Arab,
he saw the blue Mediterranean, then Maud

lying on her back on the cliff and the scarab
of the troop ship far on the roadstead. Two days' leave
before they set out, and he thought he would never

see her again, but if he did, a different life
had to be made whenever the war was over,
even if it lasted ten years, if she would wait,

not on this grass cliff but somewhere on the other
side of the world, somewhere, with its sunlit islands,
where what they called history could not happen. Where?

Where could this world renew the Mediterranean's
innocence? She deserved Eden after this war.
Past that islet out there was the Battle of the Saints.

Old Maud was ruddy as a tea-rose; once her hair
was gold as a beer-stein in firelight, but now
she'd stretch a mapped arm from her nightdress. "It's a rare

chart of the Seychelles or something." "Oh, my love, no!"
"You are my tea-rose, my crown, my cause, my honour,
my desert's white lily, the queen for whom I fought."

Sometimes the same old longing descended on her
to see Ireland. He set down his glass in the ring
of a fine marriage. Only a son was missing.

III

How fast it fades! Maud thought; the enamelled sky,
the gilded palms, the bars like altars of raffia,
even for that Madonna bathing her baby

with his little shrimp thing! One day the Mafia
will spin these islands round like roulette. What use is
Dennis's devotion when their own ministers

cash in on casinos with their old excuses
of more jobs? Their future felt as sinister as
that of that ebony girl in her yellow dress.

"There's our trouble," Maud muttered into her glass. In
a gust that leant the triangular sails of the
surfers, Plunkett saw the pride of Helen passing

in the same yellow frock Maud had altered for her.
"She looks better in it"—Maud smiled—"but the girl lies
so much, and she stole. What'll happen to her life?"

"God knows," said Plunkett, following the butterfly's
yellow-panelled wings that once belonged to his wife,
the black V of the velvet back, near the shallows.

Her head was lowered; she seemed to drift like a waif,
not like the arrogant servant that ruled their house.
It was at that moment that he felt a duty

towards her hopelessness, something to redress
(he punned relentlessly) that desolate beauty
so like her island's. He drained the foaming Guinness.

Seychelles. Seashells. One more. In the olive saucer,
the dry stones were piling up, their green pith sucked dry.
Got what we took from them, yes sir! Quick, because the

Empire was ebbing. He watched the silhouette
of his wife, her fine profile set in an oval
ivory cloud, like a Victorian locket,

as when, under crossed swords, she lifted the lace veil.
The flag then was sliding down from the hill-stations
of the Upper Punjab, like a collapsing sail;

an elephant folded its knees, its striations
wrinkling like the tea-pavilions after the Raj,
whose ebbing surf lifted the coastlines of nations

as lacy as Helen's shift. In the noon's mirage
the golden palms shook their tassels, Eden's Egypt
sank in the tinted sand. The Giza pyramids

darkened with the sharpening Pitons, as Achille shipped
both oars like rifles. Clouds of delivered Muslims
foamed into the caves of mosques, and honour and glory

faded like crested brandies. Then remorseful hymns
soared in the stone-webbed Abbey. *Memento mori*
in the drumbeat of Remembrance Day. Pigeons whirr

over Trafalgar. Helen needed a history,
that was the pity that Plunkett felt towards her.
Not his, but her story. Not theirs, but Helen's war.

The name, with its historic hallucination,
brightened the beach; the butterfly, to Plunkett's joy,
twinkling from myrmidon to myrmidon, from one

sprawled tourist to another. Her village was Troy,
its smoke obscuring soldiers fallen in battle.
Then her unclouding face, her breasts were its Pitons,

the palms' rusted lances swirled in the death-rattle
of the gargling shoal; for her Gaul and Briton
had mounted fort and redoubt, the ruined barracks

with its bushy tunnel and its penile cannon;
for her cedars fell in green sunrise to the axe.
His mind drifted with the smoke of his reverie

out to the channel. Lawrence arrived. He said:
"I changing shift, Major. Major?" Maud tapped his knee.
"Dennis. The bill." But the bill had never been paid.

Not to that housemaid swinging a plastic sandal
by the noon sea, in a dress that she had to steal.
Wars. Wars thin like sea-smoke, but their dead were real.

He smiled at the mythical hallucination
that went with the name's shadow; the island was once
named Helen; its Homeric association

rose like smoke from a siege; the Battle of the Saints
was launched with that sound, from what was the "Gibraltar
of the Caribbean," after thirteen treaties

while she changed prayers often as knees at an altar,
till between French and British her final peace
was signed at Versailles. All of this came to his mind

as Lawrence came staggering up the terrace
with the cheque finally, and that treaty was signed;
the paper was crossed by the shadow of her face

as it was at Versailles, two centuries before,
by the shade of Admiral Rodney's gathering force;
a lion-headed island remembering war,·

its crouched flanks tawny with drought, and on its ridge, grass
stirred like its mane. For a while he watched the waiter
move through the white iron shields of the white terrace.

In the village Olympiad, on St. Peter's Day,
he served as official starter with a flare-gun
borrowed from the manager of the marina.

It wasn't Aegean. They climbed no Parthenon
to be laurelled. The depot faced their arena,
the sea's amphitheatre. When one wore a crown—

victor ludorum—no one knew what it meant, or
cared to be told. The Latin syllables would drown
in the clapping dialect of the crowd. Hector

would win, or Achille by a hair; but everyone
knew as the crossing ovals of their thighs would soar
in jumps down the cheering aisle, or their marathon

six times round the village, that the true bounty was
Helen, not a shield nor the ham saved for Christmas;
as one slid down the greased pole to factional roars.

Chapter VI

I

These were the rites of morning by a low concrete
parapet under the copper spears of the palms,
since men sought fame as centaurs, or with their own feet,

or wrestlers circling with pincer-extended arms,
or oblong silhouettes racing round a white vase
of scalloped sand, when a boy on a pounding horse

divided the wrestlers with their lowering claws
like crabs. As in your day, so with ours, Omeros,
as it is with islands and men, so with our games.

A horse is skittering spray with rope for its rein.
Only silhouettes last. No one remembers the names
of foam-sprinters. Time halts the arc of a javelin.

This was repeated behind Helen's back, in the shade
of the wall. She was gossiping with two women
about finding work as a waitress, but both said

the tables was full. What the white manager mean
to say was she was too rude, 'cause she dint take no shit
from white people and some of them tourist—the men

only out to touch local girls; every minute—
was brushing their hand from her backside so one day
she get fed up with all their nastiness so she tell

the cashier that wasn't part of her focking pay,
take off her costume, and walk straight out the hotel
naked as God make me, when I pass by the pool,

people nearly drown, not naked completely, I
still had panty and bra, a man shout out, "Beautifool!
More!" So I show him my ass. People nearly die.

The two women screamed with laughter, then Helen leant
with her skirt tucked into her thighs, and asked, elbows
on her knees, if it had work in the beach restaurant

with the Chinee. They said "None." Behind her, footballers
were heading the world. Helen said: "Girl, I pregnant,
but I don't know for who." "For who," she heard an echoing call,

with *oo*'s for rings a dove moaned in the manchineel.
Helen stood up, brushing her skirt. "Is no sense at all
spending change on transport"; easing straps from each heel.

I I

Change burns at the beach's end. She has to decide
to enter the smoke or to skirt it. In that pause
that divides the smoke with a sword, white Helen died;

in that space between the lines of two lifted oars,
her shadow ambles, filly of Menelaus,
while black piglets root the midden of Gros Îlet,

but smoke leaves no signature on its page of sand.
"Yesterday, all my troubles seem so far away,"
she croons, her clear plastic sandals swung by one hand.

34

Far down the beach, where the boy had wheeled it around,
the stallion was widening. Helen heard its hooves
drumming through her bare feet, and turned, as the unreined

horse plunged with its dolphining neck, the wheezing halves
of its chest distended by the ruffling nostrils
like a bellows, as spray fanned from the punished waves,

while the boy with an Indian whoop hammered his heels
on the barrel of the belly into thick smoke
where its blur spun, whinnying, and the stallion's sound

scalded her scalp with memory. A battle broke
out. Lances of sunlight hurled themselves into sand,
the horse hardened to wood, Troy burned, and a soundless

wrestling of smoke-plumed warriors was spun
from the blowing veils, while she dangled her sandals
and passed through that door of black smoke into the sun.

And yesterday these shallows were the Scamander,
and armed shadows leapt from the horse, and the bronze nuts
were helmets, Agamemnon was the commander

of weed-bearded captains; yesterday, the black fleet
anchored there in the swift's road, in the wiry nets
thrown past the surf when the sea and a river meet;

yesterday the sightless holes of a driftwood log
heard the harp-wires on the sea, the white thunder
off Barrel of Beef, and Seven Seas and a dog

sat in a wineshop's shade; a red sail entered the
drifting tree of a rainspout, and the faint pirogue
slow as a snail whose fingers untie the reef-knots

of a common horizon left a silvery slime
in its wake; yesterday, in that sea without time,
the golden moss of the reef fleeced the Argonauts.

I saw her once after that moment on the beach
when her face shook my heart, and that incredible
stare paralyzed me past any figure of speech,

when, because they thought her moods uncontrollable,
her tongue too tart for a waitress to take orders,
she set up shop: beads, hair-pick, and trestle table.

She braided the tourists' flaxen hair with bright beads
cane-row style, then would sit apart from the vendors
on her sweet-drink crate while they bickered like blackbirds

over who had stolen whose sale, in the shadows
of the thatched hut with T-shirts and flowered sarongs.
Her carved face flickering with light-wave patterns cast

among the coconut masks, the coral earrings
reflected the sea's patience. Once, when I passed
her shadow mixed with those shadows, I saw the rage

of her measuring eyes, and felt again the chill
of a panther hidden in the dark of its cage
that drew me towards its shape as it did Achille.

I stopped, but it took me all the strength in the world
to approach her stall, as it takes for a hunter
to approach a branch where a pantheress lies curled

with leaf-light on its black silk. To stand in front of her
and pretend I was interested in the sale
of a mask or a T-shirt? Her gaze looked too bored,

and just as a pantheress stops swinging its tail
to lightly leap into grass, she yawned and entered
a thicket of palm-printed cloth, while I stood there

stunned by that feline swiftness, by the speed
of her vanishing, and behind her, trembling air
divided by her echo that shook like a reed.

Chapter VII

I

Where did it start? The iron roar of the market,
with its crescent moons of Mohammedan melons,
with hands of bananas from a Pharaoh's casket,

lemons gold as the balls of Etruscan lions,
the dead moon of a glaring mackerel; it increases
its pain down the stalls, the curled heads of cabbages

crammed on a tray to please implacable Caesars,
slaves head-down on a hook, the gutted carcasses
of crucified rebels, from orange-tiled villas,

from laurels of watercress, and now it passes
the small hearts of peppers, nippled sapodillas
of virgins proffered to the Conquistadores.

The stalls of the market contained the Antilles'
history as well as Rome's, the fruit of an evil,
where the brass scales swung and were only made level

by the iron tear of the weight, each brass basin
balanced on a horizon, but never equal,
like the old world and new, as just as things might seem.

They came out of the iron market. Achille gave
Helen back the filled basket. Helen said: *"Ba moin!"*
"Give it to me!"
                    Achille said: "Look! I not your slave!

You bound to show off for people?" Of course, she laughed
with that loud ringing laugh of hers, then walked ahead
of him. And he, feeling like a dog that is left

to nose the scraps of her footsteps, suddenly heard
his own voice ringing over the street. People turned
their heads at the shout. Achille saw the yellow dress

fold into the closing crowd. Helen never turned,
carrying the basket with both hands. Her stubbornness
made him crazy. He caught up with her. Then he tried

retrieving the basket, but she yanked it from him.
"You not my slave!" she said.
                    He said, "My hands tired."
He followed her to that part of the harbour's rim,

past the charcoal vendors, where the transports were ranged
like chariots, blunt-nosed and glaring, with the hum
of idling motors. She stopped, and in her deranged

fury screamed: "Leave me, little boy!"
Achille rammed her
against a van. He had startled a panther. Claws
raked his face in a flash; when he gripped an arm, her

fine teeth sawed his knuckles, she clawed at his good clothes,
so he, in turn, ripped the yellow dress in his rage.
Hector, whose transport this was, led her inside it,

a trainer urging a panther back to its cage.
Achille felt his body drained of all the pride it
contained, as the crowd came between him and Hector.

Achille had tears in his eyes. He could not hide it.
Her elbow moved when Hector climbed in next to her.
The van raced the harbour. Achille picked up the fruit.

II

She was not home. He remembered the morning when
he lost faith in her, and almost lost his reason
on the clearest of days. He had not told Helen

they needed quick money. Lobsters was off-season,
or diving for coral; shells was not to be sold
to tourists, but he had done this before without

getting catch himself, he knew that his luck would hold.
He was diving conchs under the lower redoubt
of the fort that ridged the lion-headed islet,

on a breezy morning, chopping the anchored skiff,
piling the conchs aboard with their frilled violet
palates, and sometimes a starfish like a stone leaf.

39

One elbow hooked on the tilted hull of the boat,
he saw, along the high wall, a yellow dress whipped
like a sail in the wind when the wind comes about,

then a fellow at the parapet's end. He slipped
slowly from the thudding hull. Helen and Hector.
He stayed underwater, the keel bumping his head,

then to the lee side, using one arm for an oar,
knowing from their height the clicking shells could be heard
because sounds travel for miles over calm water.

He tugged up the rope and eased its anchor aboard.
He paddled alongside the hull, hearing the shells
rattling on the floorboards, as his own teeth chattered.

He unwound the bow-rope and clenched it in his teeth,
with frog-shadow strokes, *In God We Troust* overhead,
the fast foam-flowers circling his head with a wreath,

and is God only to trust now, his shadow said,
because now he was horned like the island; the shells
with their hard snail-like horns were devils, their red grin

as they rolled in the salt heat over him, were hell's
lovely creatures, and his wound was Philoctete's shin.
For a long time he had sensed this thing with Hector,

now he must concentrate on carrying the conchs
safely. On certain days it had an inspector
from the Tourist Board watching the boats, and if once

they catch you, they could fine you and seize your license.
Now, when he felt he was a sufficient distance
from the redoubt, he hauled himself up with both hands.

Then, one by one, he lifted the beautiful conchs,
weighed each in his palm, considering the deep pain
of their silence, their palates arched like the sunrise,

delicate as vulvas when their petals open,
and as the fisherman drowned them he closed his eyes,
because they sank to the sand without any cries

from their parted, bubbling mouths. They were not his
property any more than Helen, but the sea's.
The thought was noble. It did not bring him any peace.

III

In this boat we were shipmates. Something had begun
to gnaw the foundations, like surf nibbling a pier,
of a love whose breezy vows assured me again

that never in my life had I been happier.
Look past that wire fence: we had said the word there,
in the shade of rattling almonds by the airport,

as if the noise of the leaves came from her blown hair,
and the salt light gusted, furrowing the waves apart,
and, three bays beyond this, in a calm cove at noon,

we swayed together in that metamorphosis
that cannot tell one body from the other one,
where a barrier reef is vaulted by white horses,

by a stone breakwater which the old slaves had built.
They joined with the slithery coupling of porpoises,
then the zebra-streaked afternoon on a white quilt,

hearing breadfruit palms scraping the roof, the noises
of the town below them, and the little crab-cries
of her parting shell, her forehead glazed with the sweat

of the bride-sleep that soothed Adam in paradise,
before it gaped into a wound, like Philoctete,
and pale slugs crawl from the sand with their newborn eyes.

And now I would wake up, troubled and inexact,
from that shallow sleep in which dreams precede sunrise,
as the vague mind cautiously acknowledges the fact

of another's outline, watching the fall and rise
of suspiring linen, like a skiff at anchor,
nodding in the dawn swell, while a sea-swift takes off

from the bow-rope, twittering, for some other shore.
And a quiet canoe is drawn, gently, with love
as one leans over and draws the wrapped shape nearer

by an invisible rope, and she parts one eye
and smiles, tapping your knuckles, and you leave her there
and stand on the morning boards of the verandah

and see between the broad leaves the small white town
below it, and a liner, and on the Morne, the
rust-roofed barracks, and insect cars crawling down.

Chapter VIII

I

In the islet's museum there is a twisted
wine-bottle, crusted with fool's gold from the iron-
cold depth below the redoubt. It has been listed

variously by experts: one, that a galleon
blown by a hurricane out of Cartagena,
this far east, had bled a trail of gold bullion

and wine from its hold (a view held by many a
diver lowering himself); the other was nonsense
and far too simple: that the gold-crusted bottle

came from a flagship in the Battle of the Saints,
but the glass was so crusted it was hard to tell.
Still, the myth widened its rings every century:

that the *Ville de Paris* sank there, not a galleon
crammed with imperial coin, and for her sentry,
an octopus-cyclops, its one eye like the moon.

Deep as a diver's faith but never discovered,
their trust in the relic converted the village,
who came to believe that circling frigates hovered

over the relic, that gulls attacked them in rage.
They kept their faith when the experts' ended in doubt.
The galleon's shadow rode over the ruled page

where Achille, rough weather coming, counted his debt
by the wick of his kerosene lamp; the dark ship
divided his dreams, while the moon's octopus eye

climbed from the palms that lifted their tentacles' shape.
It glared like a shilling. Everything was money.
Money will change her, he thought. Is this bad living

that make her come wicked. He had mocked the belief
in a wrecked ship out there. Now he began diving
in a small shallop beyond the line of the reef,

with spear-gun and lobster-pot. He had to make sure
no sail would surprise him, feathering the oars back
without clicking the oarlocks. He fed the anchor

carefully overside. He tied the cinder-block
to one heel with a slip-knot for faster descent,
then slipped the waterproof bag around his shoulders

for a money-pouch. She go get every red cent,
he swore, crossing himself as he dived. Wedged in boulders
down there was salvation and change. The concrete, tied

to his heel, pulled him down faster than a lead-
weighted, canvas-bound carcass, the stone heart inside
his chest added its poundage. What if love was dead

inside her already? What good lay in pouring
silver coins on a belly that had warmed him once?
This weighed him down even more, so he kept falling

for fathoms towards his fortune: moidores, doubloons,
while the slow-curling fingers of weeds kept calling;
he felt the cold of the drowned entering his loins.

44

Why was he down here, from their coral palaces,
pope-headed turtles asked him, waving their paddles
crusted with rings, nudged by curious porpoises

with black friendly skins. Why? asked the glass sea-horses,
curling like questions. What on earth had he come for,
when he had a good life up there? The sea-mosses

shook their beards angrily, like submarine cedars,
while he trod the dark water. Wasn't love worth more
than the coins of light pouring from the galleon's doors?

In the corals' bone kingdom his skin calcifies.
In that wavering garden huge fans on hinges
swayed, while fingers of seaweed pocketed the eyes

of coins with the profiles of Iberian kings;
here the sea-floor was mud, not corrugating sand
that showed you its ribs; here, the mutating fishes

had goggling eye-bulbs; in that world without sound,
they sucked the white coral, draining it like leeches,
and what looked like boulders sprung the pincers of crabs.

This was not a world meant for the living, he thought.
The dead didn't need money, like him, but perhaps
they hated surrendering things their hands had brought.

The shreds of the ocean's floor passed him from corpses
that had perished in the crossing, their hair like weeds,
their bones were long coral fingers, bubbles of eyes

watched him, a brain-coral gurgled their words,
and every bubble englobed a biography,
no less than the wine-bottle's mouth, but for Achille,

treading the mulch floor of the Caribbean Sea,
no coins were enough to repay its deep evil.
The ransom of centuries shone through the mossy doors

that the moon-blind Cyclops counted, every tendril
raked in the guineas it tested with its soft jaws.
Light paved the ceiling with silver with every swell.

Then he saw the galleon. Her swaying cabin-doors
fanned vaults of silvery mackerel. He caught the glint
of their coin-packed scales, then the tentacle-shadows

whose motion was a miser's harvesting his mint.
He loosened the block and shot up. Next day, her stealth
increased, her tentacles calling, until the wreck

vanished with all hope of Helen. Once more the whelk
was his coin, his bank the sea-conch's. Now, every day
he was clear-headed as the sea, wrenching lace fans

from the forbidden reef, or tailing a sting-ray
floating like a crucifix when it sensed his lance,
and saving the conch-shells he himself had drowned.

And though he lost faith in any fictional ship,
an anchor still forked his brow whenever he frowned,
for she was a spectre now, in her ribbed shape,

he did not know where she was. She'd never be found.
He thought of the white skulls rolling out there like dice
rolled by the hand of the swell, their luck was like his;

he saw drowned Portuguese captains, their coral eyes
entered by minnows, as he hauled the lobster-pot,
bearded with moss, in the cold shade of the redoubt.

I I I

Philoctete tried to make peace between them. He told
Hector that they were men, that he bore his own wound
as patiently as God allowed him, that the bad blood

between them was worse, that they had a common bond
between them: the sea. The sea that changed the cedars
into canoes, from the day they had hacked the trees

in the heights. He said, whatever a woman does,
that is her business, but men are bound by their work.
But neither listened. Like Hector. Like Achilles.

Chapter IX

I

In hurricane season, when everything is rough,
Achille ran out of money. His mate, Philoctete,
found him land-work. His canoe was a concrete trough

in Plunkett's pig-farm. A broom his oar. Through the wet,
whistling grass near the road, a sack shielding his head,
he saved money and walked six miles to the estate.

Rain hissed under black leaves, a white ground mist drifted
from the torn pastures, the hillside bamboos were broke
as he was. In the dirty gusts he missed the sea's

smell. He was glad that Plunkett still gave him a break
after Helen and the house. Cows groaned under trees,
the ochre track to the farm zigzagged in runnels

of soft, squelchy clay that fretted between his toes.
There was no sun, he was sure. No scorching gunwales
where the hot oars idled, no sea with its bleached sails.

In sucking Wellingtons he shovelled out the mash
into the steaming troughs of the jostling pen,
then jumped back from the bristling boulders that would crash

against his knees as their wooden gate swung open.
Then Achille scraped the dung-caked cement with a yard
broom, and the clogged shit spidered out into the drain

when he swung the galvanized-iron bucket hard
at the reeking wall, then hurled it harder again
in repetitious rage, the way that combers hit

a braced sea-rock, streaming. Inside, he cursed the screams
of the doomed, panicking swine matted with their shit,
their skidding trotters entered the gate of his dreams.

"I miss the light northern rain, I miss the seasons,"
Maud moaned, implying the climate lacked subtlety.
Some breeze reported the insult, since the monsoon's

anger coarsened the rain, until between the sty
and water-roped porch grew an impenetrable
jungle that drummed with increasing monotony,

its fraying lianas whipping from each gable,
the galvanized guttering belching with its roar.
Then, soaked like paper, the hills were a Chinese scroll

and she saw a subtlety where none was before.
Bamboo strokes. Wet cloud. Peasant with straw hat and pole.
Fern spray. White mist. Heron crossing fresh waterfall.

The map of heaven was breaking up in nations,
and a soggy nimbus haloed the loaded moon
when Achille saw the mare's tails, prognostications

of a grumbling sky that underlined each omen—
from the widowed veils of the indigo rainspouts
to candles of egrets screwed on a swaying branch,

then the match of lightning; in irascible knots
freckling the hot glass of the Coleman lanterns
termites singed their glazed wings and fell away as ants.

Then, next day, the stillness. And in it, the bitterns
and the gulls circling inland. Then, in the distance,
the strange yellow light. He went to buy kerosene

from Ma Kilman's crowded shop, and he was on his way back,
half-blind from her searing gas-lamp, when a blue sheen
lit the roofs and the street widened with a forked crack

of lightning igniting the egrets, splashing the palms
on the cracked plaster sky. Achille dropped the bottle.
Rain on the galvanized night. Helen in his arms.

The wind changed gear like a transport with the throttle
of the racing sea. He picked up the bottle. Before
he could, sprinting to it, fight with the rusted latch,

thudding lances of rain pinned him against the door,
but he shouldered it open, then he heard the crash
of thousands of iron nails poured in a basin

of rain on his tin roof. The cloud galleons warred
with flashing blue broadsides. Achille, soaked to the skin,
filled the lamp and lit it; he angled the brass guard

leeward of the wind and whipped off his shirt in bed.
Shadows writhed from the wick, the plantains in the yard
were wrestling to share the small roof over his head.

After a while, he got used to the heavy sound
on the galvanize. He ate cold jackfish and prayed
that his cold canoe was all right on the high sand.

He imagined the galleon, its ghost, through the frayed
ropes of the hurricane as he lowered the wick.
Hector and Helen. He lay in the dark, awake.

II

Hector wasn't with Helen. He was with the sea,
trying to save his canoe when its anchor-rope
had loosened, but sheets of black rain mercilessly

spun the bow back in the wave-troughs when he would grope
at the mooring, and in the brown, nut-littered troughs
the hull was swamping as bilge whirlpooled round his feet;

he saw how every wash crashed. Spray high as a house!
Then the long, cannon-loud boom breaking after it,
not seeing land through the rain, thinking it was close

50

from the sand-chirred water, and then he was afraid
when he saw how they were heading past the lighthouse
that spun in the gusts, with the anchor gone, the boat

keeling to the gunwale, so he shifted his weight,
he paddled hard with the short oar to come about,
but he paddled air, the wave crests brownish-white,

churning with wrenched palm-fronds; he stood up with the oar,
rocking on the keel-board, then he sat, his soul wet
and shaking. He crept to the bow, then dived ashore,

but the spinning stern clubbed him, so he stayed under
the debris to find some calm and depth, but the more
he dived, the faster the current spun him, thunder

and lightning cracked and he saw the canoe founder
without any grief; he rode a trough for a while,
paddling on his back, to measure the right rhythm

of the crests, then slid down a slow-gathering wall
like a surfer: once he caught the beat, he could swim
with the crumbling surf, not against the sea's will,

letting it spin him if it chose, even if it chose
to treat him like its garbage; then he felt the swirl
of fine sand and staggered up straight in the shallows.

III

The Cyclone, howling because one of the lances
of a flinging palm has narrowly grazed his one eye,
wades knee-deep in troughs. As he blindly advances,

Lightning, his stilt-walking messenger, jiggers the sky
with his forked stride, or he crackles over the troughs
like a split electric wishbone. His wife, Ma Rain,

hurls buckets from the balcony of her upstairs house.
She shakes the sodden mops of the palms and once again
changes her furniture, the cloud-sofas' grumbling casters

not waking the Sun. The Sun had been working all day
and would sleep through it all. After their disasters
it was he who cleaned up after their goddamned party.

So he went straight to bed at the first sign of a drizzle.
Now, like a large coalpot with headlands for its handles,
the Sea cooks up a storm, raindrops start to sizzle

like grease, there is a brisk business in candles
in Ma Kilman's shop. Candles, nails, a sudden increase in
the faithful, and a mark-up on matches and bread.

In the grey vertical forest of the hurricane season,
when the dirty sea returns the wreaths of the dead,
all the village could do was listen to the gods in session,

playing any instruments that came into their craniums,
the harp-sighing ripple of a hither-and-zithering sea,
the knucklebone pebbles, the abrupt Shango drums

made Neptune rock in the caves. Fête start! Erzulie
rattling her ra-ra; Ogun, the blacksmith, feeling
No Pain; Damballa winding like a zandoli

lizard, as their huge feet thudded on the ceiling,
as the sea-god, drunk, lurched from wall to wall, saying:
"Mama, this music so loud, I going in seine,"

then throwing up at his pun. People were praying,
but then the gods, who were tired, were throwing a fête,
and their fêtes went on for days, and their music ranged

from polkas of rain to waves dancing La Comète,
and the surf clapped hands whenever the patterns changed.
For the gods aren't men, they get on well together,

holding a hurricane-party in their cloud-house,
and what brings the gods close is the thunderous weather,
where Ogun can fire one with his partner Zeus.

Achille in his shack heard chac-chac and violin
in the telephone wires, a sound like Helen
moaning, or Seven Seas, blind as a sail in rain.

In the devastated valleys, crumpling brown water
at their prows, headlights on, passenger-vans floated
slowly up roads that were rivers, through the slaughter

of the year's banana-crop, past stiff cows bloated
from engorging mud as the antlers of trees tossed
past the banks like migrating elk. It was as if

the rivers, envying the sea, tired of being crossed
in one leap, had joined in a power so massive
that it made islands of villages, made bridges

the sieves of a force that shouldered culverts aside.
The rain passed, but people looked up to the ridges
fraying with its return, and the flood, in its pride,

entered the sea; then Achille could hear the tunnels
of brown water roaring in the mangroves; its tide
hid the keels of the canoes, and their wet gunwales

were high with rainwater that could warp them rotten
if they were not bailed. The river was satisfied.
It was a god too. Too much had been forgotten.

Then, a mouse after a fête, its claws curled like moss,
nosing the dew as the lighthouse opened its eye,
the sunlight peeped out, and people surveyed the loss

that the gods had made under a clearing-up sky.
Candles shortened and died. The big yellow tractors
tossed up the salad of trees, in yellow jackets

men straightened the chairs of dead poles, the contractors
in white helmets and slickers heard the castanets
of the waves going up the islands, moving on

from here to Guadeloupe, the beaded wires were still.
They saw the mess the gods made in one night alone,
as Lightning lifted his stilts over the last hill.

Achille bailed out his canoe under an almond
that shuddered with rain. There would be brilliant days still,
till the next storm, and their freshness was wonderful.

Chapter X

I

For Plunkett, despair came with this shitty weather,
from the industrious torrents of mid-July
till the farm was drubbed to a standstill. This year, the

rain was an unshifting thicket, the branched sky
grew downwards like mangroves, or an immense banyan.
The bulbs dangled weakly from the roof of the pens,

their cords sticky with flies, till he, like everyone
else, watched the drifts, hating the separate silence
that settled his labourers when their work was done.

He saw that their view of him would always remain
one of patronage; his roof was over their heads,
as they sat disconsolately watching the rain

erode and dissolve the mounds of Maud's garden-beds,
their eyes glazed and clouded with some forgotten pain
from the white shambles of lilies, the dripping boards

of rope-twisted water blown from the leaking pen,
while Maud sat embroidering her tapestry of birds
in the lamplit house which each horizontal gust

blew farther from him. He saw her in the windows
and felt she was drifting away, just like the ghost
of the drowned galleon. He bolted up to the house.

He stayed in the house. The ginger tom boxed its paws
at the yarn-knitting window. Hogs ran to slaughter
like infantry tired of trenches and shovels,

and rain-maddened lilies chose a death by water,
like pregnant virgins in Victorian novels.
Maud rescued some. In rain hat and yellow slicker,

she bent over their beds in the gentler drizzles;
then the beds would darken, the drizzles grow thicker
in an even heavier downpour than the last.

Trees and power poles fell. Lamps came on in the house.
A winter besieged them with limp weeklies and tea.
Beyond the orchids she watched the grey-shawled showers

cross the grey lawn, then go down towards the grey sea.
By the crystal teardrop lamp she'd brought from Ireland,
humming then stopping, then humming. Settling the bulbs

of saved lilies in vases with her leaf-veined hand.
Seychelles. Seashells. He watched her, then, with glottal gulps
that maddened her, sucked his tea. He felt murderous

as the monsoon when she started playing some tripe
about "Bendemeer's stream," each chord binding the house
with nerves of itching ivy; he crammed in his pipe,

then bit it erect, and in a raw, sodden rage
strode to the unshawled piano and slammed the lid,
missing her fingers. Maud waited. She closed the page

of *Airs from Erin* and, very carefully, hid
it under the velvet of the piano stool,
brushed past him with her shawl, and climbed up the slow stairs,

tugging at her fingers. No fool like an old fool,
the Major raged. The window was streaming with tears,
but none came. When? It was the old wound in his head.

Rubbish. Easy excuse. He never blamed the war.
It was like original sin. Then the Major heard
someone knocking carefully. The voice said: "Major?

Major, we going," and left. The ginger uncurled
from the dark sofa. He lifted him carefully,
placed him by the window to look out on this world

the way he no longer did. Then, his heart full, he
went up, eased the door: Sleeping. But she never slept
with one elbow over her eyes. Sorrow dissolved

him, and he sat on the bed, and then both of them wept
the forgiving rain of those who have truly loved.
It seemed long as the season, and then the rain stopped.

II

Once the rains passed they took the olive Land Rover
round the shining island, up mornes with red smudges
of fresh immortelles with old things to discover;

the deep-green crescents held African villages
that, over centuries, had roofed their shacks with tins,
erected a square stone church, until by stages,

the shacks would creep down the ridges to become towns.
That was how History saw them. He studied the course
that it offered: the broken roads, the clear rivers

that congealed to sepia lagoons, from which some case
of bilharzia would erupt in kids whose livers
caught the hookworm's sickle. Pretty, dangerous streams.

Their past was flat as a postcard, and their future,
a brighter and flatter postcard, printed the schemes
of charters with their poverty-guaranteed tour.

In the frayed whisks of the vanished storm he felt his
own scalp, freckled, with its skeins of thinning hair,
but sunshine broke through the misty precipices

with a double rainbow that turbanned La Sorcière,
the sorceress mountain with a madras kerchief
and flashing spectacles. They called her Ma Kilman

because the village was darkened by their belief
in her as a *gardeuse*, sybil, obeah-woman
webbed with a spider's knowledge of an after-life

in her cracked lenses. She took Holy Communion
with Maud sometimes, but there was an old African
doubt that paused before taking the wafer's white leaf.

The Rover whined up the Morne till they saw, below
a shelf of sunshot asphalt, the expansive plunge
of Cul-de-Sac valley and the soaked indigo

serration of peaks. A sky, loaded like a sponge,
dabbed at, then dried the defiant beads of moisture
on the levelled bananas with their fecal smell

of new mud; but their irrigation ditches were
channels of light and the oval potholes small
mirrors of blueing cloud that the tires shattered,

that almost instantly reglazed their reflection,
until the storm's green ruin no longer mattered,
and the sparkling road only increased affection

when they watched the sunlight redefining Roseau's
old sugar-factory roof. The road climbed the bay,
as a cool wind thatched the bamboos like osiers,

urging them with light tongues downward to Anse La Raye,
chattering with expectation at the young sprouts
that would spring from the storm. Their delight was strengthened

by boys racing the Rover with half-naked shouts,
offering them bananas, until the bends straightened
and left them gasping for breath against the wet trees,

till others sprouted from grass around the next bend;
then the sea widened its blue around Canaries,
and the road, coiling with ochre precipices,

was like a rope that bound them, much closer even
than the hurricane, by its azure silences,
the way lianas knot their inseparable vine

around two tree trunks sometimes, or a mast grows leaves
in the heart of a forest, binding every vein,
rooted in the island for the rest of their lives.

The horns of the island were peaks split asunder
by a volcanic massif. Through ferns, Soufrière
waited under springs whose smoke signalled the thunder

of the dead. It was a place where an ancient fear
increased as he neared it. Holes of boiling lava
bubbled in the Malebolge, where the mud-caked skulls

climbed, multiplying in heads over and over,
while the zircon gas from the flues climbed the bald hills.
This was the gate of sulphur through which he must pass,

singeing his memory, though he pinched his nostrils
until the stench faded into verdurous peace,
like registering skulls in the lime-pits of Auschwitz.

The wound closed in smoke, then wind would reopen it,
a geyser would jet its gas through a cracked fissure
the way that steam suddenly hissed from the bonnet

of the uncapped radiator, scalding his face
if he didn't leap clear. He filled the cooling ring
from a stream in the ferns. Then they went on climbing

around larger and greener ferns, their wide fronds
large as a fan belt's, passing the old sulphur mine
with its rusted wheel, its hawsers of lianas,

where a Messrs. Bennett & Ward, his countrymen,
in 1836 went home to England as
bush and high taxes foreclosed their wild enterprise.

Wreaths of funereal moss draped their endeavour.
A huge wheel's teeth locked in rust. What had stopped their schen
Quarrels over money? Had one caught a fever,

and, yellow as that leaf, in his delirium
babbled of an alchemy that could turn sulphur
gold, while his partner dabbed the cold sweat of a dream

from his forehead? Had they had another offer
somewhere on the outer boundaries of freedom
and free enterprise that came with an empire?

What was their force? How would they extract the mineral
from the mine and transport it? Transport it to where?
Or had they run out of money and that was all,

until fever grass and bush foreclosed the idea
and their banks were weed? He saw the sprocketed wheel
gritting its teeth at the sulphur that still lay there.

In the sharp blue heights beyond them there were orchids
springing from the side-paths. Sometimes, a resinous
woodsman would startle them, his bag full of snake-heads

to flog to Der Guva'ment. He walked without noise,
a shaft of light angling the floor of the forest
without shaking the ferns, his soles quiet as moss.

Through stumps of brown teeth he pointed out the hillcrest
with gaping, precipitous valleys, where smoke rose
from a charcoal pit, and under the smoke, the lines

of a white, amnesiac Atlantic, then with a bow,
and a patois blessing with old African signs,
as soundless as light on the road they watched him go.

England seemed to him merely the place of his birth.
How odd to prefer, over its pastoral sites—
reasonable leaves shading reasonable earth—

these loud-mouthed forests on their illiterate heights,
these springs speaking a dialect that cooled his mind
more than pastures with castles! To prefer the hush

of a hazed Atlantic worried by the salt wind!
Others could read it as "going back to the bush,"
but harbour after crescent harbour closed his wound.

There was a lot in the island that Maud hated:
the moisture rotting their library; that was the worst.
It seeped through the shawled piano and created

havoc with the felt hammers, so the tuner cost
a regular fortune. After that, the cluttered light
on the choked market steps; insects of any kind,

especially rain-flies; a small, riddling termite
that cored houses into shells and left windows blind;
barefoot Americans strolling into the banks—

there was a plague of them now, worse than the insects
who, at least, were natives. Turbanned religious cranks
urging sisters with candles to the joy of sects,

the velocity of passenger transports on
uncurbed highway, comets that hurtled out of sight
and brought a flash to the heart; the darkening monsoon

of merciless July with patches of sunlight
mercurial as Helen, the slanted, almond eyes
of her ebony beauty. And then an elate

sunrise would flood Maud's garden, pouring relentless
light in angelic lilies, yellow chalices
of morning-glories, and Queen Anne's seraphic lace.

Just then he saw the butterfly pinned to a blade
like a nervous pennant. She had followed him here.
The dilating panels pulsed to his trembling blood,

the wing-folded palms in their parody of prayer;
then they would widen, like the eyes of Maud's scissors
following a seam. Was he condemned to see her

every time one twinkled up out of Maud's garden?
What did she want? For History to exorcise her
theft of the yellow frock? Did she crave his pardon?

After a while the happiness grew oppressive.
Only the dead can endure it in paradise,
and it felt selfish for so long. He felt as if

the still, lemon panels were painted with her eyes.
There's too much poverty below us. Every leaf
defines its limits. All roots have their histories.

"It's so still. It's like Adam and Eve all over,"
Maud whispered. "Before the snake. Without all the sin."
And their peace was so deep, they sat in the Rover

listening to the bamboos. He switched on the engine
and they bucketed, wobbling over rain-ruts, hurled
on the groaning springs down to the flat, real world.

Chapter XI

I

Pigs were his business. These people were not resigned
to living with garbage, drifting in numbed content
as the filth narrowed the drains. They had not designed

the Attic ideal of the first slave-settlement,
with sea-grapes for olives and black philosophers
with clouds over their elbows. They had not laid out

narrow-gauge pipes for buckets, but none for sewers.
They had not sucked the cane till sugar was played out.
Empires were swinish. These had splendid habits

of cleanliness, compulsively sweeping yards dry
with their palm-brooms. Encouraged to screw like rabbits
by estates who liked labour and, naturally, by

a Church that damned them to hell for contraceptives.
But they waxed their tables, flailed their beaten laundry
on the river-rocks; there were ikons in their lives—

the Virgin, the Virgin Lamp, the steps lined with flowers,
and they learnt quickly, good repairers of engines
and fanatical maids. Helen had kept the house

as if it were her own, and that's when it all begins:
when the maid turns into the mistress and destroys
her own possibilities. They start to behave

as if they owned you, Maud said. This was the distress
of the pale lemon frock, which Helen claimed Maud gave
her but forgot. He stayed out of it, but that dress

had an empire's tag on it, mistress to slave.
The price was envy and cunning. The big church, the
middens by cloudy lagoons, kids racing like piglets.

If History saw them as pigs, History was Circe
with her schoolteacher's wand, with high poles at the fêtes
of saint-day processions past al fresco latrines.

So Plunkett decided that what the place needed
was its true place in history, that he'd spend hours
for Helen's sake on research, so he proceeded

to the whirr of enormous moths in the still house.
Memory's engines. The butterfly dress was hers,
at least her namesake's, in the Battle of the Saints.

During this period his life grew increasingly
bookish and slippered, like a don's. He stayed in. Maud
wondered about his wound. When she took in his tea

he nodded towards the side-table, and this made
her leave him with his ziggurat of books, his charts,
and the balsa fleet he carved with a small scalpel,

while she sipped hers in the arched shade with her orchids.
Dusk darkened the pots, an allamanda's bell
bronzed in the sky-fire, then melted into night.

Dennis was still at work when she took her tray in.
The desk was dark, except for a green pool of light
cast on its baize by a lamp curved like a heron.

She sat on a chair beside him. He didn't speak,
and the tea was untouched. One finger traced the line
of some map, and the nose, with its man-o'-war's beak,

skimmed the white page. She had never felt more alone.
A light rain had washed the stars. They looked very close.
Maud sighed, then went upstairs. She could feel the white sea

losing its white noise slowly, drawing the windows;
she studied the map on one forearm, then briskly
loosened the bridal knot of the mosquito net,

then stretched it to the corners of the tautened pane,
carried the straw basket with the bright spools in it
down to the divan, her needles swift as his pen.

She thought: I dreamed of this house with woods around it,
with trees I'd read of, whose flowers I'd never seen.
Part of a barracks, with no noise to surround it

but cicadas chattering like my sewing-machine.
I loved the young teak with bodies clean as birches
in light that freckled the leopard shade of the path,

when martins at dusk with their crisscrossing stitches
would sew the silk sky, or preen around the birdbath.
I saw it when we first came. Unapproachable

cliff on one side, but its ledges a nesting place
for folding herons and gulls, and my teak table
with its lion-claw legs and its varnished surface

spread with fine scalloped linen, white as the sea's lace,
and ringing crystal, with a fresh wreath of orchids
like Remembrance Day, at my brass candlestick's base,

in Dennis's honour mainly, and the place cards
near the bone-china of my huge lily-pad plates.
Have I put on airs, to think of dinner-candles

and flags and lances since we slow-marched down the aisle
under crossed swords? Then, my tureen with thick handles
hefted by Helen, her cap white as my napkins

rolled in their crested holders. She'd set it in place,
and step back in shadow that blent with her fine skin's.
What a loss, that girl! I ladled the fragrant steam

of my stew in thick portions, the dark full of fireflies
that never catch the leaves. It's as clear as a dream,
but more real. Well, folks lived for centuries

like this with candles and airs on the piano,
the love-songs fading over a firefly sea,
their mouths round as the moon over a black canoe

like the one I smiled at today: *In God We Troust*.
But then we all trust in Him, and that's why we know
the peace of a wandering heart when it is housed.

Chapter XII

I

Our house with its bougainvillea trellises,
the front porch gone, was a printery. In its noise
I was led up the cramped stair to its offices.

I saw the small window near which we slept as boys,
how close the roof was. The heat of the galvanize.
A desk in my mother's room, not that bed, sunlit,

with its rose quilt where we were forbidden to sit.
Pink handbills whirred under their spinning negative
and two girls stacked them from their retractable bed

as fast as my own images were reprinted
as I remembered them in an earlier life
that made the sheets linen, the machines furniture,

her wardrobe her winged, angelic mirror. The hum
of the wheel's elbow stopped. And there was a figure
framed in the quiet window for whom this was home,

tracing its dust, rubbing thumb and middle finger,
then coming to me, not past, but through the machines,
clear as a film and as perfectly projected

as a wall cut by the jalousies' slanted lines.
He had done a self-portrait, it was accurate.
In his transparent hand was a book I had read.

"In this pale blue notebook where you found my verses"—
my father smiled—"I appeared to make your life's choice,
and the calling that you practise both reverses

and honours mine from the moment it blent with yours.
Now that you are twice my age, which is the boy's,
which the father's?"
                              "Sir"—I swallowed—"they are one voice."

In the printery's noise, and as we went downstairs
in that now familiar and unfamiliar house,
he said, in an accent of polished weariness,

"I was raised in this obscure Caribbean port,
where my bastard father christened me for his shire:
Warwick. The Bard's county. But never felt part

of the foreign machinery known as Literature.
I preferred verse to fame, but I wrote with the heart
of an amateur. It's that Will you inherit.

I died on his birthday, one April. Your mother
sewed her own costume as Portia, then that disease
like Hamlet's old man's spread from an infected ear,

I believe the parallel has brought you some peace.
Death imitating Art, eh?"
                              At the door to the yard,
he said, "I grew grapes here. Small, a little sour,

still, grapes all the same."
                              "I remember them," I said.
"I thought they died before you were born. Are you sure?"
"Yes." The furred nap like nettles, their globes' green acid.

"What was Warwick doing, transplanting Warwickshire?"
I saw him patterned in shade, the leaves in his hair,
the vines of the lucent body, the swift's blown seed.

I I

Out on the sidewalk the sunlight drained like the print
of a postcard flecked with its gnawing chemical
in which there was light, but with a sepia tint,

even on Grass Street with our Methodist chapel.
We passed under uprights with fretworks on their eaves,
mansards with similar woodwork, their verandahs

shuttered at both corners by half-cranked jalousies
through which pale cousins peered or a half-cracked aunt, as
if from the madhouse or a convent. Windows

framed their unshifting lives. During the hot, long day
they kept changing posts near which they leant, their elbows
jutting from a ledge, elbows as well known as they

were, or with a white head dipping in a rocker
while the black town walked barefoot and deafening bells
pounded the Angelus; but none saw the walker

in his white suit, their reveries were somewhere else,
they looked on their high-brown life as a souvenir
with a dried Easter palm, its amber sweets, its carts

horse-drawn, rubbing their beads and muttering *Veni,
Creator* to velvet cushions with embroidered hearts.
As iron bells ruled the town, and the poui flowers fell.

I I I

It was one. We passed the brown phantoms in white-drill
suits, some with pith-helmets whom the Angelus sent
back to work after lunch, suits rippled by the grille

of shade made by the long-stemmed pillars as we went
past them, the asphalt so hot that it was empty.
Heat waves rippled over it and one or two cars

pumped their bulb-horns and waved as they rattled by.
Then we came to a green square cut in smaller squares.
And the light from a bluer postcard filled its sky,

and it seemed, from his steps, that water sprang in plumes
from the curled, iron-green fountain at its centre,
though its gates were shut under pluming cabbage-palms,

a paradise I had to believe to enter.
But I did not ask him about the other life,
because the white shadow I had made from my mind

was vague in its origin and thin as belief,
unsinged as an Easter lily, fresh as the wind,
its whisper as soft as a pavement-scratching leaf.

Chapter XIII

I

"I grew up where alleys ended in a harbour
and Infinity wasn't the name of our street;
where the town anarchist was the corner barber

with his own flagpole and revolving Speaker's seat.
There were rusted mirrors in which we would look back
on the world's events. There, toga'd in a pinned sheet,

the curled hairs fell like commas. On their varnished rack,
The World's Great Classics read backwards in his mirrors
where he doubled as my chamberlain. I was known

for quoting from them as he was for his scissors.
I bequeath you that clean sheet and an empty throne."
We'd arrived at that corner where the barber-pole

angled from the sidewalk, and the photographer,
who'd taken his portrait, and, as some think, his soul,
leant from a small window and scissored his own hair

in a mime, suggesting a trim was overdue
to my father, who laughed and said "Wait" with one hand.
Then the barber mimed a shave with his mouth askew,

and left the window to wait by his wooden door
framed with dead portraits, and he seemed to understand
something in the life opposite not seen before.

"The rock he lived on was nothing. Not a nation
or a people," my father said, "and, in his eyes,
this was a curse. When he raged, his indignation

jabbed the air with his scissors, a swift catching flies,
as he pumped the throne serenely round to his view.
He gestured like Shylock: 'Hath not a Jew eyes?'"

making his man a negative. An Adventist,
he's stuck on one glass that photograph of Garvey's
with the braided tricorne and gold-fringed epaulettes,

and that is his other Messiah. His paradise
is a phantom Africa. Elephants. Trumpets.
And when I quote Shylock silver brims in his eyes."

I I

"Walk me down to the wharf."
                               At the corner of Bridge
Street, we saw the liner as white as a mirage,
its hull bright as paper, preening with privilege.

"Measure the days you have left. Do just that labour
which marries your heart to your right hand: simplify
your life to one emblem, a sail leaving harbour

and a sail coming in. All corruption will cry
to be taken aboard. Fame is that white liner
at the end of your street, a city to itself,

taller than the Fire Station, and much finer,
with its brass-ringed portholes, mounting shelf after shelf,
than anything Castries could ever hope to build."

The immaculate hull insulted the tin roofs
beneath it, its pursers were milk, even the bilge
bubbling from its stern in quietly muttering troughs

and its humming engines spewed expensive garbage
where boys balanced on logs or, riding old tires,
shouted up past the hull to tourists on the rails

to throw down coins, as cameras caught their black cries,
then jackknife or swan-dive—their somersaulting tails
like fishes flipped backwards—as the coins grew in size

in the wobbling depth; then, when they surfaced, fights
for possession, their heads butting like porpoises,
till, like a city leaving a city, the lights

blazed in its moving rooms, and the liner would glide
over its own phosphorus, and wash hit the wharves
long after stewards had set the service inside

the swaying chandeliered salons, and the black waves
settle down to their level. The stars would renew
their studded diagrams over Achille's canoe.

From here, in his boyhood, he had seen women climb
like ants up a white flower-pot, baskets of coal
balanced on their torchoned heads, without touching them,

up the black pyramids, each spine straight as a pole,
and with a strength that never altered its rhythm.
He spoke for those Helens from an earlier time:

"Hell was built on those hills. In that country of coal
without fire, that inferno the same colour
as their skins and shadows, every labouring soul

climbed with her hundredweight basket, every load for
one copper penny, balanced erect on their necks
that were tight as the liner's hawsers from the weight.

The carriers were women, not the fair, gentler sex.
Instead, they were darker and stronger, and their gait
was made beautiful by balance, in their ascending

the narrow wooden ramp built steeply to the hull
of a liner tall as a cloud, the unending
line crossing like ants without touching for the whole

day. That was one section of the wharf, opposite
your grandmother's house where I watched the silhouettes
of these women, while every hundredweight basket

was ticked by two tally clerks in their white pith-helmets,
and the endless repetition as they climbed the
infernal anthracite hills showed you hell, early."

III

"Along this coal-blackened wharf, what Time decided
to do with my treacherous body after this,"
he said, watching the women, "will stay in your head

as long as a question you have no right to ask,
only to doubt, not hate our infuriating
silence. I am only the shadow of that task

74

as much as their work, your pose of a question waiting,
as you crouch with a writing lamp over a desk,
remains in the darkness after the light has gone,

and whether night is palpable between dawn and dusk
is not for the living; so you mind your business,
which is life and work, like theirs, but I will say this:

O Thou, my Zero, is an impossible prayer,
utter extinction is still a doubtful conceit.
Though we pray to nothing, nothing cannot be there.

Kneel to your load, then balance your staggering feet
and walk up that coal ladder as they do in time,
one bare foot after the next in ancestral rhyme.

Because Rhyme remains the parentheses of palms
shielding a candle's tongue, it is the language's
desire to enclose the loved world in its arms;

or heft a coal-basket; only by its stages
like those groaning women will you achieve that height
whose wooden planks in couplets lift your pages

higher than those hills of infernal anthracite.
There, like ants or angels, they see their native town,
unknown, raw, insignificant. They walk, you write;

keep to that narrow causeway without looking down,
climbing in their footsteps, that slow, ancestral beat
of those used to climbing roads; your own work owes them

because the couplet of those multiplying feet
made your first rhymes. Look, they climb, and no one knows them;
they take their copper pittances, and your duty

from the time you watched them from your grandmother's house
as a child wounded by their power and beauty
is the chance you now have, to give those feet a voice."

We stood in the hot afternoon. My father took
his fob-watch from its pocket, replaced it, then said,
lightly gripping my arm,
                              "He enjoys a good talk,

a serious trim, and I myself look ahead
to our appointment." He kissed me. I watched him walk
through a pillared balcony's alternating shade.

BOOK TWO

Chapter XIV

I

The midshipman swayed in the coach, trying to read.
He knew that the way to fortify character
was by language and observation: the Dutch road

striped with long poplar shadows in the late after-
noon, the weight of the man in his coach, a sunbeam
changing sides on the cushion, a spire's fishhook

luring a low shoal of clouds like silvery bream
towards it; the light gilding the spine of his book,
the stale smell of canals in the red-thatched farmer

who glowered and swung like a lantern on the seat
opposite, with the marsh-breath of an embalmer,
a wire-coop of white chickens between his feet,

each boot as capacious as those barges crossing
the Lowland reaches at dusk. The Dutch were grossing
a fortune in the Northern Antilles, and he

wondered if the farmer knew this with night closing
round his flambent Flemish nose. Admiral Rodney
had asked for the smartest midshipman possible,

who needed only one thing, a good memory,
so he was assigned to work his way to The Hague,
but in the roundabout way of all those people,

the higher the post the more their orders were vague.
He leant back in the coach, inspecting the twilight
ranked in darkening poplars, between which the farmer

glared at him. In a box on the roof, its ropes tight,
its brass clasp flashing, was his blue uniform; a
sword folded in it. He turned to the farmer's face.

He had counted the clustered berries on the nose,
noted the eyebrows' haystacks, the dull canal gaze
of his reflection, the forehead's deep-ploughed furrows,

the bovine leisure with which he turned away eyes
stupefied by distances. Swaying on one knee,
an ochre jug gurgled. From this the farmer swallowed,

then heeled the cork shut with a ham-sized palm, only
to wriggle it again with one thumb to a loud
squeak that seemed to surprise him with every mile.

The stomach's rippling orb enraged the squire,
who averted each offer with a hardening smile
at this bulk, obese and turgid as his Empire.

Were it not for the war he might have loved the place;
even with its ribbed windmills' skeletal rattle,
for its orange-roofed farms hidden among poplars,

wheels with crystal weirs, its black-mapped, creamy cattle
grazing their long shadows. The fields were prosperous
and lied of peace. From them, horizontal fire

lit an enormous cloud, then its changing towers
were crossed by unlucky rooks, and a touched spire
withdrew from the field, as dusk pricked its first flowers.

Under a sucked-out sun, like a lemon lozenge
on a blue Delft plate, he counted the black crosses
of shipping, the steeples, and the immense

clouds over the port emptied as if by a plague.
The farmer grunted, not to him but to the chickens
between his huge boots, and boasted in Dutch: "The Hague."

A spy sent through the Lowlands, he was to observe
from certain ports the tonnage, direction, and mass
of Dutch merchantmen; the arms they shipped in reserve

to American colonies through St. Eustatius,
an island bristling with contraband; then embark
to Plymouth to serve with Rodney. A florin moon

showed him the footman lowering his chest in the dark
of the wharves. He tipped his hat to the footman
and gave him a coin. He was a very thorough

and observant young officer with an honour-
able career ahead of him, but a bit raw.
His name was Plunkett, his vessel *The Marlborough*.

Gunpowder and stores were shipped to St. Eustatius
from these innocent, moonlit harbours, in support
of French aid to the colonies; with slow paces,

the sea-chest hidden, he walked the edge of the port
as the moonlight amazed him, its milk-white brilliance
pouring from dark pewter clouds. It shone with such force

he could read his palm by it, and from this distance,
the curled brass names of the vessels under their prows.
He memorized them, closing his eyes, reprinted

their silhouettes like an etching. These merchantmen
sold guns not only to North American agents
but to British merchants selling their countrymen

to profitable conflict. The intelligence
would be used by the Admiral at home, to wreak
massive revenge not only on the Dutch islands

but on the French island bastion of Martinique,
with its sheltering harbour where the whole French fleet
could muster. For some reason, under the immense

clouds, he remembered the coop between the feet
of the farmer, with its uncomplaining chickens
waiting to be sacrificed, resigned to their fate.

His forked shadow aped him, scribbling its own report,
when a cry from the Night Watch froze it. They both hid
between huge kegs of gunpowder that lined the port,

while the startled moon, like a hunted hare, scurried
through the bare masts as leafless as its winter hills
to a snowcrest of powdery cloud. The hare stood

with its limp forepaws, ears pronged, its quivering nostrils
veering like a compass till it found the black wood
under whose rigging the Night Watch crunched like hunters

climbing with shouldered guns towards it. The hare's face
of the frightened moon, as they searched with their lanterns
and ready muskets, made his pulse echo the pace

of the hare's heart up those hills he had hunted once,
he muffled his heartbeat with one paw. A cloud capped
his own frightened face, and the moon's. The hare crept down

into the cloud with its white tuft. The midshipman kept
low behind a wine-barrel, a huge demijohn,
and moved like the crippled hare back towards its den,

leaving drops on the snow, heart like a lantern
that the hunters might see, or wine-drops that redden
a snowy tablecloth, to where his sword was hidden.

His intelligence helped. After the Dutch defeat
on the islet facing Martinique, a great redoubt
was being prepared. Rodney was building a fort.

III

The slaves watched the Redcoats running between the trees,
dispersing like blossoms when the poinciana
rattles its hanging bandoliers in the breeze

as the thunderheads ignite with no cannoneer.
Battles were natural as storms; they needed no cause.
A common enemy bound captive to captor.

They clapped as the soldiers scrambled to the redoubts,
and their hot palms longed for lances in that rapture
of men before war, till a fusillade of shouts

burst from the apoplectic, sunburnt engineers.
They got back to their job of hauling the cannon
that hung halfway up the cliff over the white noise

of the sea-lace. It was bound like a cadaver
lowered at a sea-burial, with this difference—
that the roped body was rising from the water

in iron resurrection, inch by squeaking inch
from the rusty hawser, dangerously swaying,
while two slaves locked and kept the wheel-handle of the winch

from whirring backwards and others watched the fraying
ropes that smoked from the strain. If a single knot frayed,
the cannon would hit the cliff and its weight unravel

the balance and the strain on their shoulders too great
as the weight increased and the cannon would travel
straight down to the sea, carrying slaves and soldiers

with it. There was fear and pride in their work now
and Achille's ancestor cursed his pain-locked shoulders,
tilting his body for purchase, locking his jaw

like the winch of the wheel until his temples hurt,
but he passed on the engineer's orders: "More! More!"
and felt the little avalanches of loose dirt

under his soles. The cries of black warrior ants
passed in a chain as they lifted the iron log
towards the crest of the trees, so he changed their response

to a work-song they knew, hauling a long pirogue
up from their river, and between beats his commands
varying softly, then the groans between the counting,

and, higher than pain, they let the ropes saw their hands
till they bled on the hemp, and the cannon mounting,
mounting, until its mouth touched the very first branch,

like an iguana climbing, entering the trees.
And their hands sprung up like branches: slaves, engineers,
they embraced one another separately, in tears.

They leapt in the air, they drummed with their blurring heels,
they loosened and flipped the ropes, and the hawser's tails
wriggled up the precipice. In its iron wheels

the iron lizard sat fixed towards the French sails.
That was their victory. Some paused to watch the foam
chaining the black rocks below them, and thought of home.

It was then that the small admiral with a cloud
on his head renamed Afolabe "Achilles,"
which, to keep things simple, he let himself be called.

Chapter XV

In the channel with three islets christened "Les Saintes,"
in a mild sunrise the ninth ship of the French line
flashed fire at *The Marlborough*, but swift pennants

from Rodney's flagship resignalled his set design
to break from the classic pattern. *The Marlborough*
declined engagement and veered from the cannonade;

reading the pennants, she crossed the enemy's trough,
her sister frigates joining the furrow she made.
You have seen pelicans veer over pink water

of an April bay. So, stem-to-stern, Rodney's force
in a bracing gust followed *The Marlborough*; but, since
the wind grew too light, both fleets were tacking off-course

and closing in at three or four knots from the wind's
changing sides; so close that all their cannoneers could
read the other's arc of ignition, hear the shout

before the recoil, and see the splintering wood,
then close-fire muskets, like cicadas in drought,
or stones that crack from a fisherman's beach-fire.

The midshipman felt the hull coming hard about;
the Admiral had wanted some hands below, before
the close fighting. His order had to be obeyed.

A malevolent flower of smoke continued past dawn
on the brightening horizon. He heard the deep roar
of the boatswain, the gunner's "Aye!" From her squadron

a French frigate coming close had been hit. She bore
down on *The Marlborough*, the young midshipman peered
at her smoke-shawled beauty, and thought there was no war

as courtly as a sea-battle; her white sails steered
towards him, her embrochures spitting fire
while black veils of fury billowed from her beaked head;

for this he had watched the gulls from his ploughed shire,
the canvas on one shoulder, and the deadly ride
through marsh lowlands. Observation is character,

so he watched her wallowing in her wounded pride
with her loosened stores, he heard feet pounding the board
of the upper-deck, and slid, as his vessel tried

to avoid ramming. He held on, reached for his sword,
when *The Marlborough* shuddered to the dying groan
of the cracking mainmast, a gommier, a split elm,

its leaves like collapsing canvas, covering the ground.
He grabbed air as the helmsman wheeled hard at the helm,
then the sky showed through a hole. Then it vomited

a wave through the wooden maw, spewing its debris
of splinters and—God knows why—bottles; as she passed
he read her ornate italics: *Ville de Paris*.

He was making for the ladder that led them up
to the deck, sword drawn in one hand. With the other
he was hoisting himself on the rail when the ship

foundered again and another huge wave poured through
the hole, and this time its wash rapidly mounted
in the cabin, spinning him from the ladder against

the wall opposite, and as hard as he tried
to wade in its whirlpool of debris, the next wave sent
him against his own sword. It was a fatal wound

but he pulled out the sword. Then the wash thudded him
on the roof of the cabin, the surge spun him round
as he swallowed water with no floor under him.

Once the breach was drained and the direction altered
and the shorn mast stripped, the pouring breach was secured.
They found him face downwards, still holding to the sword.

From the hull of the *Ville de Paris*, wine-bottles
bobbed in the wake, crimson blood streamed from the wood
as they drifted in the mild current from the battle's

muffled distance. The casks and demijohns' blood
stained the foam faintly, and now one of them settles
on the sea-floor, its pyrite crusted and oblate

with the sea-blown, distended glass. Huge tentacles
rolled it as a cat boxes its prey. Then it was left—
a chalice hoisted by a diver's rubber claws.

Chapter XVI

Plunkett's ances-tree (his pun) fountained in blossoms
and pods from a genealogical willow
above his blotter's green field. One pod was the Somme's.

It burst with his father's lungs. Then a pale yellow
asterisk for a great-uncle marked Bloemfontein.
At the War Office he'd paid some waxworks fellow

to draw flowers for battles, buds for a campaign.
The cold-handed bugger'd done it for a fortune.
Undertaker's collar, bald as a snooker-ball,

as hunched as a raven, he plucked titles in turn
from their cliffs of gilt ledgers, picking with his bill
from Agincourt to Zouave, returning to where

he found blue blood in the Plunketts. The Major
voiced no objection. But why Scots? Why a claymore
with a draped tartan? And, when the willow faded

into a dubious cloud, he smiled. To pay more,
naturally, and he did. A carved, scrolled shield waited
at the willow's base, his name and hyphen

for a closing date, then a space for son and heir.
"No heir," he told the mummy from Madame Tussaud,
who believed he had dropped an aitch. "I mean 'No. Here,' "

snapped the Major, pointing to where the blank place showed
on the waiting shield. "No heir: the end of the line.
No more Plunketts."

The crow wrote it on the design.

I I

An evening with the Plunketts: he marking cannons
by their Type, Trunions, Bore, Condition, Size, Weight,
in a marbled ledger, by order of Ordnance,

Cipher—GR. III, GR>IV, Site, Silhouette, Date,
nib scratching the page, beaking the well for a word,
Maud with her needle, embroidering a silhouette

from Bond's *Ornithology*, their quiet mirrored
in an antique frame. Needlepoint constellations
on a clear night had prompted this intricate thing,

this immense quilt, which, with her typical patience,
she'd started years ago, making its blind birds sing,
beaks parted like nibs from their brown branch and cover

on the silken shroud. Mockingbirds, finches, and wrens,
nightjars and kingfishers, hawks, hummingbirds, plover,
ospreys and falcons, with beaks like his scratching pen's,

terns, royal and bridled, wild ducks, migrating teal,
pipers (their fledgling beaks), wild waterfowl, widgeon,
Cypseloides Niger, l'hirondelle des Antilles

(their name for the sea-swift). They flew from their region,
their bright spurs braceleted with Greek or Latin tags,
to pin themselves to the silk, and, crying their names,

88

pecked at her fingers. They fluttered like little flags
from the branched island, budding in accurate flames.
The Major pinched his eyes and turned from the blotter—

green as a felt field in Ireland—and saw her mind
with each dip of her hand skim the pleated water
like a homesick curlew. Frogs machine-gunned the wind.

Dun surf cannonaded. A star furled its orchid,
faded and fell. The hours drowsed like centuries
mesmerized by the clock's metronome. Maud lifted

and shook the silk from her lap, smoothing her knees.
She did not look up. He watched as the beaked scissors made
another paper cutout. A scratch in his throat

made him cough, softly. Softly the pendulum swayed
in its ornate mahogany case; he was tired,
but her hair in the aureole cast by the shade

never shifted. How often had he admired
her hands in the half-dark out of the lamplit ring
in the deep floral divan, diving like a swift

to the drum's hoop, as quick as a curlew drinking
salt, with its hover, skim, dip, then vertical lift.
Tonight he shuddered like the swift, thinking,

This is her shroud, not her silver jubilee gift.
His vision was swimming with fathom-depths, degrees
bubbling with zeroes on the old nautical charts;

he pinched his eyesockets. Cannons flashed from his eyes.
He dropped the dividers, tired of fits and starts;
the exact line of engagement was hard to find,

whimsical cartographers aligned the islands
as differently as dead leaves in a subtle wind.
He bent to the map, rubbing his scalp with his hands.

III

Once, after the war, he'd made plans to embark on
a masochistic odyssey through the Empire,
to watch it go in the dusk, his "I" a column

with no roof but a pediment, from Singapore
to the Seychelles in his old Eighth Army outfit,
calculating that the enterprise would take him

years, with most of the journey being done on foot,
before it was all gone, a secular pilgrim
to the battles of his boyhood, where they were fought,

from the first musket-shot that divided Concord,
cracking its echo to some hill-station of Sind,
after which they would settle down somewhere, but Maud

was an adamant Eve: "It'll eat up your pension."
But that was his daydream, his pious pilgrimage.
And he would have done it, if he had had a son,

but he was an armchair admiral in old age,
with cold tea and biscuits, his skin wrinkled like milk,
a gawky egret she stitched in her sea-green silk.

Chapter XVII

Now, whenever his mind drifted in detachment
like catatonic noon on the Caribbean Sea,
Plunkett recited every billet, regiment,

of the battle's numerological poetry;
he learnt eighty ships of the line, he knew the drift
of the channel that day, and when the trade wind caught

the British topsails, and a deep-draught sigh would lift
his memory clear. At noon, he climbed to the fort
as his self-imposed Calvary; from it, the cross

of the man-o'-war bird rose. He heard the thunder
in the cannonading caves, and checked the pamphlet
from the museum, ticking off every blunder

with a winged V, for the errors in either fleet.
In his flapping shorts he measured every distance
with a squared, revolving stride in the khaki grass.

One day, at high noon, he felt under observance
from very old eyes. He spun the binoculars
slowly, and saw the lizard, elbows akimbo,

belling its throat on the hot noon cannon, eyes slit,
orange dewlap dilating on its pinned shadow.
He climbed and crouched near the lizard. "Come to claim it?"

the Major asked. "Every spear of grass on this ground
is yours. Read the bloody pamphlet. Did they name it
Iounalo for you?"
                    The lizard spun around

to the inane Caribbean. Plunkett also.
"Iounalo, twit! Where the iguana is found."
He brought it for the slit eye to read by the glow

of the throat's furious wick.
                              "Is that how it's spelt?"
The tongue leered. The Major stood, brushed off his khaki
shorts, and rammed the pamphlet into his leather belt.

"Iounalo, eh? It's all folk-malarkey!"
The grass was as long as his shorts. History was fact,
History was a cannon, not a lizard; De Grasse

leaving Martinique, and Rodney crouching to act
in the right wind. Iounalo, my royal arse!
Hewañorra, my hole! Was the greatest battle

in naval history, which put the French to rout,
fought for a creature with a disposable tail
and elbows like a goalie? For this a redoubt

was built? And his countrymen died? For a lizard
with an Aruac name? It will be rewritten
by black pamphleteers, History will be revised,

and we'll be its villians, fading from the map
(he said "villians" for "villains"). And when it's over
we'll be the bastards! Somehow the flaring dewlap

had enraged him. He slammed the door of the Rover,
but, driving down the cool aisle of casuarinas
like poplars, was soothed by the breakwater. In a while

he was himself again. He was himself or as
much as was left. Innumerable iguanas
ran down the vines of his skin, like Helen's cold smile.

II

He kept up research in Ordnance. The crusted wrecks
cast in the armourer's foundry, the embossed crown
of the cannon's iron asterisk: *Georgius Rex*,

or Gorgeous Wrecks, Maud punned. In that innocence
with which History fevers its lovers, a black wall
became its charred chapel, and a mortar-seized fence

of green stones near the Military Hospital
bent his raw knees for a sign; when he came outside
from a pissed tunnel, his face had the radiance

of a convert. How many young Redcoats had died
for her? How many leaves had caught yellow fever
from that lemon dress? He heard the dry bandolier

of the immortelle rattling its pods. "Forever"
was the flame tree's name, without any reason,
since it marched like Redcoats preceding the monsoon.

How was the flower immortal when it would flare
only in drought, a flag of the rainy season,
of gathering thunderheads, each with its scrolled hair

wigged like an admiral's? Then he found the entry
in pale lilac ink. *Plunkett*. One for the lacy trough.
Plunkett? His veins went cold. From what shire was he?

On what hill did he pause to watch gulls follow a plough,
seabag on one shoulder, with his apple-cheeked sheen?
This was his search's end. He had come far enough

to find a namesake and a son. *Aetat xix.*
Nineteen. Midshipman. From the horned sea, at sunrise
in the first breeze of landfall, drowned! And so, close

his young eyes and the ledger. Pray for his repose
under the wreath of the lilac ink, and the wreath
of the foam with white orchids. Bless my unbelief,

Plunkett prayed. He would keep the namesake from Maud.
He thought of the warm hand resting on the warm loaf
of the cannon. And the crown for which it was made.

Chapter XVIII

I

The battle fanned north, out of sight of the island,
out of range of the claim by native historians
that Helen was its one cause. An iguana scanned

the line of a sea that settled down to silence
except for one last wash over the breakwater
as the French fleet worked its way up to Guadeloupe

with Rodney heeling them hard. What he was after
was such destruction it would be heard in Europe—
masts splintering like twigs and fed to the fire

in George the Third's hearth—in which the sun's gold sovereign
would henceforth be struck in the name of one Empire
only in the Caribbean, gilding the coast

of the Eastern Seaboard from Georgia to Maine.
The Dutch islands were in Rodney's pocket and the cost
to the New England colonies was the French fleet

racing like mare's tails, each ship a dissolving ghost
of canvas turned cloud, until that immense defeat
would block their mutinous harbours from arms and men.

The Major made his own flock of V's, winged comments
in the margin when he found parallels. If she
hid in their net of myths, knotted entanglements

of figures and dates, she was not a fantasy
but a webbed connection, like that stupid pretense
that they did not fight for her face on a burning sea.

He had no idea how time could be reworded,
which is the historian's task. The factual fiction
of textbooks, pamphlets, brochures, which he had loaded

in a ziggurat from the library, had the affliction
of impartiality; skirting emotion
as a ship avoids a reef, they followed one chart

dryly with pen and compass, flattening an ocean
to paper diagrams, but his book-burdened heart
found no joy in them except their love of events,

and none noticed the Homeric repetition
of details, their prophecy. That was the difference.
He saw coincidence, they saw superstition.

And he himself had believed them. Except, once,
when he came into the bedroom from the pig-farm
to pick up his chequebook, he was fixed by her glance

in the armoire's full-length mirror, where, one long arm,
its fist closed like a snake's head, slipped through a bracelet
from Maud's jewel-box, and, with eyes calm as Circe,

simply continued, and her smile said, "You will let
me try this," which he did. He stood at the mercy
of that beaked, black arm, which with serpentine leisure

replaced the bangle. When she passed him at the door
he had closed his eyes at her closeness, a pleasure
in that passing scent which was both natural odour

and pharmacy perfume. That victory was hers,
and so was his passion; but the passionless books
did not contain smell, eyes, the long black arm, or his

knowledge that the island's beauty was in her looks,
the wild heights of its splendour and arrogance.
He moved to the coiled bracelet, rubbing his dry hands.

I I

The bracelet coiled like a snake. He heard it hissing:
Her housebound slavery could be your salvation.
You can pervert God's grace and adapt His blessing

to your advantage and dare His indignation
at a second Eden with its golden apple,
henceforth her shadow will glide on every mirror

in this house, and however that fear may appall,
go to the glass and see original error
in the lust you deny, all History's appeal

lies in this Judith from a different people,
whose long arm is a sword, who has turned your head
back to her past, her tribe; you live in the terror

of age before beauty, the way that an elder
longed for Helen on the parapets, or that bed.
Like an elder trembling for Susanna, naked.

He murmured to the mirror: No. My thoughts are pure.
They're meant to help her people, ignorant and poor.
But these, smiled the bracelet, are the vows of empire.

Black maid or blackmail, her presence in the stone house
was oblique but magnetic. Every hour of the day,
even poking around the pigs, he knew where she was;

he could see her shadow through the sheets of laundry,
and since she and her shadow were the same, the sun
behind her often made their blent silhouette seem

naked, or sometimes, carrying a clean basin
of water to the bleaching stones, she wore the same
smile that made a drama out of every passing.

The village was bounded by a scabrous pasture
where boys played cricket. On its Caribbean side
was a cemetery of streaked stones and the tower

of a Norman church where the old river died.
Like reeds in the old lagoon the French in their power
had lifted a forest of masts with Trojan pride.

When the pages of sea-grapes in their restlessness
lifted a sudden gust, through asterisks of rain,
he climbed the small hill of garbage, and on its mess

he stood there, measuring out the site with his cane
and a small map he had found that was falling apart
from its weathered spine in the back of the library.

From this he had made his own diagram, a chart
that he measured as two thousand steps from the sea,
which concluded in the mound's elegiac rampart.

In the rain-blotted dusk, what was he raking for,
poking with his cane there among the ruined shoes,
a question on a seething heap, raking some more

when something shone, metallic? What thing did he lose?
The midden was a boredom of domestic trash
whose artifacts showed nothing but their simple sins,

as clearly as rainwater in a calabash,
cracked as the crescent moons of enamel basins.
Boys watched the white man's inexhaustible patience

chasing the curious piglets away from his work,
which was to prove that the farthest exclamations
of History are written by a flag of smoke,

from Carthage, from Pompeii, from the burial mound
of antipodal Troy. Midden built on midden;
by nature men always chose the same dumping ground

or an ancestral grove, and what lay hidden
under the heap of waste was the French cemetery
when the place was an outpost, facing Gros Îlet.

But this was also her village, this was where she
walked and swam on its beach, this was her parapet.
The midden proved to have been the capital port.

But then she had been the glory of nations once,
the shoes and basins of Troy. Imperial France
lay in his palm: two brass regimental buttons.

Chapter XIX

I

Now he could roar out Breen's encomium by rote
because of his son's sacrifice in a battle.
The apple of his pride bobbed in his wattled throat,

with a cannonade of a cough, something between a death-rattle
and a wavering sob. He taught Maud to say it by heart:
"When we consider the weighty interest involved in the issss . . .

ue . . ." (there was always a spray of spittle with this part,
as the sibilants reared with an adder's warning hiss),
"*Whereby the mighty projects of the coalesced powers*

*were annihilated and Britain's dominion on the seas
secured . . .*" Maud recited it to the yellow allamandas
as if they were fleurs-de-lys, as her clicking secateurs

beheaded them into a basket and up the stone stairs.
He found his Homeric coincidence.
                                        "Look, love, for instance,
near sunset, on April 12, hear this, the *Ville de Paris*

struck her colours to Rodney. Surrendered. Is this chance
or an echo? Paris gives the golden apple, a war is
fought for an island called Helen?"—clapping conclusive hands.

He saw the boy's freckled face, the forehead turning
under the thatch of red hair, the blue eyes, plum lips,
and, without the full cotton middy, the burning

shoulders raw from the heat, and the other midships
ranged on these iron steps. Some, inaudibly, laughed,
facing the sun's lens. They were buffing sword-handles

with cleaning fluid, like the droppings of a swift
on a statue's head, or like Maud's dinner-candles,
all of them wondering how much time they had left

in the sun near the shade of the tanks, each feature
repeating the same half-naked, shadowy grin,
in a sepia album; he crouched with them there,

holding his Enfield, a tin basin to piss in
under his raw knee and the grinning boy was where
they all were now. In their stone waves, the home shire

of the sun-crossed Armistices, where a bugler
with a golden cord suddenly snaps its tassels
under an arm. And Mortimer, and Glendower,

and Tumbly and Scott, their sadly echoing souls
faded over the desert with its finest hour,
no longer privates, midshipmen, but grinning shells.

O Christ have mercy on them all! Christ forgive him,
for mockery of the midshipmen from whom home
could never be drilled, courage was out of fashion,

just as the faith had gone out from every hymn,
till only rhythm remained; and what was rhythm
if over their swinging arms there was not passion,

not only for England, but some light that led them
beyond their drill-patterns like rooks? For him, they shone
the sword hilts with rags. Not honour, but service;

the bugler's summons not for brazen renown,
but it threaded their veins, privates and officers,
like Maud's needles. For it, a young Plunkett would drown.

II

Since the house was on the very ground where buglers
had stood on the steps of the barracks, summoning
half-dressed soldiers from sleep, when frosted dew was

silvering the grass, they all came shouting and running
down the brick arches to the powder magazine,
because French sails were sighted on the horizon,

cries multiplied in Plunkett. Mute exclamations
of memory! Assembled ranks shouting their name
as they wriggled on braces, stamping "Sah!" Rations

for the cannon's mouth, the black iron lizard's flame.
Now, one of the longest barracks was the college.
He'd park in the Rover, watching young Neds and Toms

swinging their shadows but giggling at the rage
of their soprano sergeant. Fathering phantoms
like the name in the ledger, their numbers remained

when dusk slanted the barrack's echoing arches,
with Scott's cry and Tumbly's, all the ones he had trained
before these cadets. The mace, flung high in marches

through the wooden streets, then flung higher overhead
and caught like an exclamation! In the night wind
the palms swayed like poplars along the Dutch marshes.

III

As the fever of History began to pass
like the vision of the island's luminous saint,
he saw, through the Cyclops eye of the gliding glass,

over wooden waves of a naval aquatint,
a penile cannon emerge from its embrochure.
Able semen, he smiled. He had gone far enough.

He leant back, frowning, on the studded swivel chair;
then, with one hand, he spun the crested paper-knife
that stopped dead as a compass, making an old point—

that the harder he worked, the more he betrayed his wife.
So he edged the glass over the historic print,
but it magnified the peaks of the island's breasts

and it buried stiff factions. He had come that far
to learn that History earns its own tenderness
in time; not for a navel victory, but for

the V of a velvet back in a yellow dress.
A moth hung from the beam, reversed, and the Major
watched the eyed wing: watching him, a silent witness.

He remembered the flash of illumination
in the empty bar—that the island was Helen,
and how it darkened the deep humiliation

he suffered for her and the lemon frock. Back then,
lightning could lance him with historic regret
as he watched the island through the slanted monsoon

that wrecked then refreshed her. Well, he had paid the debt.
The breakers had threshed her name with the very sound
the midshipman heard. He had given her a son.

The great events of the world would happen elsewhere.
There were those who thought his war had been the best war,
that the issues were nobler then, the cause more clear,

their nostalgia shone like the skin on his old scar.
There were dead Germans, machine-gunned near the hotels.
In History, he'd had a crypto-Fascist master

who loved German culture above everything else,
from the Royal House of Hanover to Kaiser
Wilhelm; he had given, as one of his essays,

"A few make History. The rest are witnesses."
Beethoven's clouds enrapt him, and Hermann Hesse's
punctilious face. His essay had won first prize.

Chapter XX

I

By the witness of flambeaux-bottles, by the sweat
of distorted faces screaming for Workers' Rights
on the steps of the iron market, Philoctete

peered at each candidate through the blinding arc-lights
to cresting gusts of applause for an island torn
by identical factions: one they called Marxist,

led by the barber's son, the other by Compton
which Maljo, who took him there, called Capitalist.
In the rumshop he asked Maljo which to support.

"Me," Maljo said, "them two men fighting for one bone."
He'd pay his deposit, he'd rent Hector's transport
and buy batteries for a hand-held megaphone.

His party was launched at the depot. The ribbon
was cut by the priest, its pieces saved for later
Christmas presents. In the village where he was born,

a tall cynic heckled: "Scissors can't cut water!"
"*Ciseau pas ça couper del'eau!*" meaning the campaign
was a wasted effort; the candidate addressed

his barefoot followers with a glass of champagne
to toast their trust, and a megaphone which he pressed
for its crackling echo, deafening those two feet

away from him. Since every party cost money,
he marched his constituents clapping up the street
to the No Pain Café to start the ceremony.

There Seven Seas sang for them, there his good compère
Achille promised to canvas for him in the depot
during domino games. A new age would begin.

You could read its poster by the sodium glow
of a lamppost at night. Its insomniac grin
plastered on a moonlit wall with its cheering surf,

while the charter yachts slept and crabs counted the sand,
with his registered name: F. DIDIER, BORN TO SERVE,
its sign: a broken chain dangling from a black hand.

"Bananas shall raise their hands at the oppressor,
through all our valleys!" he screamed, forgetting to press
the megaphone button. They named him "Professor

Static," or "Statics," for short, the short-circuit prose
of his electrical syntax in which he mixed
Yankee and patois as the lethargic Comet

sputtered its sparked broadsides when the button was fixed.
As Party Distributor he paid Philoctete,
who limped in the vanguard with handouts while the crowd

shouted "Statics!" and Maljo waved. He, who was once
fisherman-mechanic, felt newly empowered
to speak for those at the backs of streets, all the ones

idling in breadfruit yards, or draping the bridges
at dusk by the clogged drains, or hanging tired nets
on tired bamboo, for shacks on twilight ridges

in the wounding dusk. Their patience was Philoctete's.
By the Comet's symbol he knew their time had come,
and what Philo could contribute as a member

was the limp that drove his political point home
as he hopped to Maljo's funereal timbre,
haranguing the back streets, forgetting the button.

"Ces mamailles-là!" Statics shouted, meaning *"Children!"*
Then Hector would tap his knee with: "The mike not on."
"Shit!" said the Professor with usual acumen.

II

His cripple bounced ahead, distributing pamphlets,
starching them to cars and government buildings marked:
POST NO BILLS; then Philoctete sank in the Comet's

leopard upholstery. In the country, they parked
by a rumshop. He'd lead the clapping while Statics
shook hands, or gave a lollipop at a standpipe

to a toothless sibyl; he was learning the tricks.
To his black Lodge suit he added a corncob pipe
and MacArthur's vow as he left: *"Moi* shall return."

Power went to Statics's head. He felt like the Pope
in his bulletproof jeep; he learnt how to atone
for their poverty, waving from the parted door

of the gliding Comet, past neglected sections,
nodding, dipping two fingers stuck with a power
that parted the sea of their roaring affections.

"This island of St. Lucia, quittez moin dire z'autres!
let me tell you is heading for unqualified
disaster, ces mamailles-là, pas blague, I am not

joking. Every vote is your ticket, your free ride
on the Titanic: a cruise back to slavery
in liners like hotels you cannot sit inside

except as waiters, maids. This chicanery!
this fried chicanery! Tell me if I lying.
Like that man hopping there, St. Lucia look healthy

with bananas and tourists, but her soul crying,
'tends ça moin dire z'autres, tell me if I lying.
I was a fisherman and it lancing my heart

at neglection-election to see my footman
wounded by factions that tearing him apart.
The United Force will not be a third party

between two parties, one Greek and the other Trojan,
both fighting for Helen: LP and WWPP,
only United Love can give you the answers!"

They drove through Roseau. He said: "Are you hearing me?"
"Yes," Hector said. "I not sure 'bout the bananas,"
pressing the button. The Comet trawled its echo

through the emerald valleys and the indigo hills,
up rutted shortcuts and their paradisal view
of rain-weathered villages with cathedrals—

the heaven of the priest's and politician's vow,
and the blue sea burst his heart again and again
as Philoctete sat, with the pamphlets in his lap,

watching the island filing backwards through the pane
of his wound and the window, from Vieuxfort to Cap.
He was her footman. It was her burden he bore.

Why couldn't they love the place, same way, together,
the way he always loved her, even with his sore?
Love Helen like a wife in good and bad weather,

in sickness and health, its beauty in being poor?
The way the leaves loved her, not like a pink leaflet
printed with slogans of black people fighting war?

III

The Comet stopped again to let off Philoctete.
They were crawling through Castries, block by crowded block.
He limped through the crowds, as the crackling megaphone

moved past the market steps.
                              "Ces mamailles-là, nous kai rock
Gros Îlet, *the United Force giving a block-
orama till daybreak on Friday until cock*

put down his saxophone and violon en sac.
*All your contributions are welcome in aid of
Professor Statics's United Force. Peace and love!"*

The night of the Statics Convention Blocko it rained,
it drenched out his faith in the American-style
conviction that voters needed to be entertained.

Statics toured the fête's debris with a wounded smile.
Beaded bouquets of balloons, soggy paper-hats,
rain-corrugated posters, the banner across

two balconies, the cardboard cartons of pamphlets,
were history this Saturday. It was their loss,
not his. A career prophesied by the Comet's

having a ball. He laughed. He rehired Philoctete
to clean up the hall first, then distribute the wet
balloons to the kids. Then he watched him disconnect

the bunting's wrinkling face from a stepladder
with a pronged pole. It sagged like a kite to the street.
That, from the candidate, was his final order,

pointing a warm beer in his shorts and sandalled feet.
He hugged Philoctete, who wept for their defeat.
He left as a migrant-worker for Florida.

Chapter XXI

I

The jukebox glowed in Atlantic City. Speakers
bombarded the neon of the No Pain Café.
The night flared with vendors' coalpots, the dull week, as

it died, exploded with Cadence, Country, Reggae.
Stars burst from the barbecues of chicken and conch,
singeing the vendors' eyes. Round their kerosene lamp

the children's eyes widened like moons until they sank
in the hills of their mothers' laps. Frenetic DJs
soared evangelically from the thudding vamp

of the blockorama,
          "This here is Gros Îlet's
night, United Force, garçon, we go rock this village
till cock wake up!"
          The rumshops, from Midnight Hour,

Keep Cool, No Pain Café, to the high Second Stage,
with its Christmas lights winking, with decibel power
shattered the glass stars. Tourists, in seraphic white,

floated through the crowding shadows, the cooking smells,
the domino games by gas lanterns. Helen's night.
The night Achille dreaded above everything else.

She sprinkled and ironed a dress.
          "Is the music,
the people, I like." Once the sun set on Fridays,
he grew nauseous with jealousy, watching the thick

breadfruit leaves viciously darken as the cafés
switched their doors open, and the first policemen barred
the street off with signs. After an early supper

he sat in the frame of the back door to the yard
watching her head, in the shower he'd built for her
from brand-new galvanize, streaming from the white foam

with expensive shampoo, and, when it disappeared,
came back, the mouth parted, the eyes squeezed with delight.
She stepped over the wet stones smiling, and she nodded

to him silent on the back step with Plunkett's towel
holding her beaded nakedness. He said nothing.
He watched the lathered stones, even they seemed to smell

of her clean feet and her long arms' self-anointing.
In the bedroom, she started again—he should come,
but she soon gave that up. The pipe was still trickling,

so he got up and locked it. If Seven Seas was home
he would sit with him in front of the pharmacy
with its closed door, and describe some parts of the fête

to Seven Seas, whom he envied, who couldn't see
what was happening to the village. At the bent gate
he paused. No. He would go and sit with the canoes

far up the beach and watch the star-crowned silhouette
of the crouched island. Even there the DJ's voice
carried over the shallows' phosphorescent noise.

Or he watched her high head moving through the tourists,
through flying stars from the coalpots, the painted mouth
still eagerly parted. Murder throbbed in his wrists

to the loudspeaker's pelvic thud, her floating move.
She was selling herself like the island, without
any pain, and the village did not seem to care

that it was dying in its change, the way it whored
away a simple life that would soon disappear
while its children writhed on the sidewalks to the sounds

of the DJ's fresh-water-Yankee-cool-Creole.
He sat on *In God We Troust* under black almonds,
listening to the Soul Brothers losing their soul;

the sandy alleys would go and their simple stores,
the smell of fresh bread drawn from its Creole oven,
its flour turned into cocaine, its daughters to whores,

while the DJs screamed,
                    "WE MOVIN', MAN! WE MOVIN'!"
but towards what? Those stars were too fixed in heaven
to care, but sometimes he wished that he was as far

as they were. The young took no interest in canoes.
That was longtime shit. Once it came from Africa.
And the sea would soon get accustomed to the noise.

He watched a falling star singe the arc of its zone
and traced the comet as its declining vector
hissed out like a coal in the horizon's basin

over the islet, and he trembled for Hector,
the title he gave his transport. Bright Helen
was like a meteor too, and her falling arc

crossed over the village, over some moonlit lane
with its black breadfruit leaves. Every life was a spark,
but her light remained unknown in this backward place,

falling unobserved, the way he watched the meteor
at one in the morning track the night of her race,
then fade, forgotten, as sunrise forgets a star.

II

Dominus illuminatio mea, Egypt delivered
back to itself. India crumpling on its knees
like a howdah'd elephant, all of the empowered

tide and panoply of lances, Gurkhas, Anzacs, Mounties
drained like a bath from the bunghole of Eden's Suez,
or a back-yard canal. In Alexandria, at the raven's hour,

clouds of the faithful hunch at the muezzin's prayers,
with the hymn of mosquitoes, deserts whence our power
withdrew, Himalayan hill-stations where the millipede

enters and coils, like a lanyard around a flagpole,
and the rat scuttles in straw, jungles where a leopard
narrows its gaze to sleep on a crumbling uphol-

stered sofa, while chickens climb the stairs. The crest
of the bookmark was under his thumb, the frontispiece
signed by a boy's hand. *D. Plunkett.* He laid him to rest

between the water-stained pages as he shut the book.
Dominus illuminatio mea, O Lord, light of my life.
He turned his head towards Maud, but she did not look

up from her needle. He fiddled with the paper-knife
on the blotter. He had won the prize for an essay
on the Roman Empire. In those days, history was easy.

He arched like the cat, and went to the verandah
as Maud looked up once. The Major counted the stars
like buttons through the orchids; they were the usual wonder.

He heard the contending music, on one side from the bars
of the village, thudding; on the other, across black water,
the hotel's discotheque. At that very moment Achille was

studying a heaven whose cosmology had been erased
by the crossing. He was trying to trace the armature
of studs and rivets where the constellations are placed,

but for him they were beads on an abacus, no more.
From night-fishing he knew the necessary ones,
the one that sparkled at dusk, and at dawn, the other.

All in a night's work he saw them simply as twins.
He knew others but would not call them by their given
names, forcing a silvery web to link their designs,

neither the Bear nor the Plough, to him there was heaven
and earth and the sea, but Ursa or Plunkett Major,
or the Archer aiming? He tried but could not distinguish

their pattern, nor call one Venus, nor even find
the pierced holes of Pisces, the dots named for the Fish;
he knew them as stars, they fitted his own design.

I I I

"What?"
          She was draping the silk slip on a hanger,
twisting it skillfully. She turned her breasts away.
Down the deep ravine of her shoulders, his anger

drained like the soapy water over the pathway
of stones he had placed there, where her small footprints dried.
It was still moonlight, and the moonlight filled the sheen

of the nightgown she entered like water as her pride
shook free of the neck. He saw the lifted wick shine
on the ebony face, and the shadow she made

on the wall. Now the shadow unpinned one earring,
its head tilted, and smiled. It was in a good mood.
It checked its teeth in a mirror, he watched it bring

the mirror close to its eyes. The blocko was done.
It was so quiet in the village, he heard the stars
click like its earrings when the shadow put them down.

He turned his face to the wall. Whoever she was,
however innocent her joy, he couldn't take it
anymore. A transport passed, and in the silence

he felt his heart sicken, watching her as she brushed
her hair slowly and stopped. And Achille saw Helen's
completion for the first time. He saw how she wished

for a peace beyond her beauty, past the tireless
quarrel over a face that was not her own fault
any more than the full moon's grace sailing dark trees,

and for that moment Achille was angrily filled
with a pity beyond his own pain. There was peace
in the clouds, and the moon in a silk-white nightgown

stood over him.
                    "What?" he said. "What make you this whore?
Why you don't leave me alone and go fock Hector?
More men plough that body than canoe plough the sea."

The lance of his hatred entered her with no sound,
yet she came and lay next to him, and they lay quietly
as two logs laid parallel on moonlit sand.

He heard the fig-trees embracing and he smiled
when the first cock cuckolded him. She found his hand
and held it. He turned. She was asleep. Like a child.

Chapter XXII

Shortly after, she moved in with Hector. She moved
everything while he was fishing but a hairpin
stuck in her soap-dish. To him this proved

that she would come back. Stranger things than that happen
every day, Ma Kilman assured him, in places
bigger than Gros Îlet. When he walked up a street,

he stuck close to the houses, avoiding the faces
that called out to him from doorways. He passed them straight.
Gradually he began to lose faith in his hands.

He believed he smelt as badly as Philoctete
from the rotting loneliness that drew every glance
away from him, as stale as a drying fishnet.

He avoided the blind man with his black, knotted hands
resting on the cane; he avoided looking at
a transport when it approached him, in case, by chance,

it was Hector driving and should in case she sat
on the front seat by him; the van that Hector bought
from his canoe's sale had stereo, leopard seat.

The Comet, a sixteen-seater passenger-van,
was the chariot that Hector bought. Coiled tongues of flame
leapt from its sliding doors. Each row was a divan

of furred leopardskin. Because of its fiery name
under an arching rocket painted on its side,
the Space Age had come to the island. Passengers

crammed next to each other on its animal hide
were sliding into two worlds without switching gears.
One, atavistic, with its African emblem

that slid on the plastic seats, wrinkling in a roll
when the cloth bunched, and the other world that shot them
to an Icarian future they could not control.

Many accepted their future. Most were prepared
for the Comet's horizontal launching
of its purring engine, part rocket, part leopard,

while Hector, arms folded, leant against the bonnet
like a gum-chewing astronaut. He would park it
first in rank. Every old woman who got on it—

there was always one quarrelling from the market—
would pause and look at the painted flames with *"Bon Dieu!
Déjà?"*—meaning "Hell? Already?" Once, one remarked,

"All I see is tiger-skin, yes. So let us prey."
And pray they did, when Hector rammed the flaming door
shut, then his own side harder as he touched the charm

of a fur monkey over the dashboard altar
with its porcelain Virgin in flowers and one arm
uplifted like a traffic signal to halt. Her

statue lurched, swaying, the passengers clutched the skins
as Hector pedalled the clutch in roaring reverse,
and the wharf flashed past them quicker than all their sins

as the old woman clawed the rosary in her purse
and begged the swaying Virgin not to forget her
at the hour of our death, and sudden silence

descended on the passengers and on Hector,
because it was here he had stepped between Helen's
fight with Achille. Why he had bought this chariot

and left the sea. He believed she still loved Achille,
and that is why, through palm-shadows, the leopard shot
with its flaming wound that speed alone could not heal.

He was making no money. The trips were too short.
He liked wide horizons. Soon the Comet was known
through the sea of banana fields to the airport,

making four trips a day when most transports made one,
hearing his fame shouted on the way to Vieuxfort,
and sometimes, just for a change, coming back empty,

he leant back on the leopardskin, the stereo on
his favourite station: Country. He liked the falling
scarves of the sunset saying goodbye to the sea

the way he had left it. Curving around Praslin
he thought of his *camerades* hauling their canoes
and the dusk thatching their sheds without any noise.

The months revolved slowly like the silk parasols
at college cricket-matches; sometimes cicadas
past the edge of the pavilion burst into applause

for a finished stroke. By five, the fielders' shadows
on the slanted field were history, and the light
for that moment turned as tea-tinted as the prose

of old London journals, *The Sphere*, *The Tatler*, *The
Illustrated London News*; then quietly, the white
languid dominion of the water-lily in the heat

behind the reed-barred gates of Maud Plunkett's pond
was floating into darkness, the clouds were dying,
the field sparked with green fireflies, like sparks flying

from an evening coalpot, the singeing stars.
Low over the mangoes, close over the hills, like fire
under a tin, the sun went out, and the horizon

enclosed the schooners, the canoes, and an empire
faded with one last, spastic green flash, but so soon
they hardly noticed. The Plunketts quietly continued,

parades continued, cricket resumed, and the white feathers
of the proconsul's pith-helmet, and the brass and red
of the fire engines. Everything that was once theirs

was given to us now to ruin it as we chose,
but in the bugle of twilight also, something unexpected.
A government that made no difference to Philoctete,

to Achille. That did not buy a bottle of white kerosene
from Ma Kilman, a dusk that had no historical regret
for the fishermen beating mackerel into their seine,

only for Plunkett, in the pale orange glow of the wharf
reddening the vendors' mangoes, alchemizing the bananas
near the coal market, this town he had come to love.

Chapter XXIII

I

It was a rusted port with serrated ridges
over which clouds carried grey crocus-bags of rain;
past its heyday as a coaling-station. Dredges

deepened its draft and volcanic silt would remain
on its bed, but liners, higher than the iron
lance of the market, whitened the harbour and rose

above the Customs. Every noon, a carillon
sprinkled its yellow petals above a morose
banyan. The Church of Immaculate Conception

was numbering the Angelus. With lace frills on,
balconies stood upright, as did the false pillars
of the Georgian library; each citizen

stood paralyzed as the bell counted the hours.
A dozen halos of sound down through the ages
confirmed the apostles. At store-counters, shoppers

crossed themselves with the shopgirls; tellers in cages
stopped riffling their own notes with one wet fingertip
drying before it moved on to turn the next leaf.

The streets held statues. A traveller off a ship
could have sauntered through that Pompeii of their belief
made by the ash of the Angelus, like St. Pierre,

whose only survivor had been a prisoner
who watched the volcano's powder mottle the air
across the channel to blacken milk and flour.

Then the statues stirred, iron-shop blinds rippled down,
the banks closed for an hour, the entire town
went home for lunch, to come back on the stroke of one.

11

Maud heard the carillon, faint in the wiry heat
over the hot harbour. She watched a lizard crawl down
the fly screen. She took off her damp gardening hat

and lay on the faded couch, she loosed her bodice
and blew down to her heart. It was cool in the shade
of the stone porch hung with her baskets of orchids.

She stared at the slope of the lawn down to the farm
where grass withered in scabs. Then, a canoe. Headed
for Africa, probably, passing her royal palm.

Shadows were sloping down the desiccated lawn
from the bougainvillea hedge. The morning-glory
was wilting. The sea-grape's leaves were vermilion,

orange, and rust, their hues a *memento mori*
as much as autumn's, when their crisp pile would be raked
by limping Philoctete. Smoke wrote the same story

since the dawn of time. Smoke was time burning. It snaked
itself into a cloud, the wrinkled almond trees
grew older, but lovely, the dry leaves were baked

like clay in a kiln. Their brightness was a disease
like the golden dwarf-coconuts. It was the same
every drought. The sea hot. The sea-almond aflame.

III

A liner grew from the Vigie promontory,
white as a lily, its pistil an orange stack.
She crept past the orchids. At the morning-glory

she stopped in mid-channel, then slowly turned her back
on the island. By dusk, she'd be a ghost like all
her sisters, a smudge on a cloud. Maud marked their routes:

the cost of a second-class berth from Portugal
to Southampton, then Dublin, but the cheapest rates
staggered Dennis. She soon grew used to the liner

moored to the hedge. A girl was coming up the trace,
pausing for breath, and though the light was behind her
and the garden glaring, by the slow, pelvic pace

that made men rest on their shovels cleaning the pens
and the gardener pause from burning leaves on the lawn,
a heap in his hands, Maud knew that gait was Helen's,

but the almond eyes were hooded in the smooth face
of arrogant ebony. Maud tugged off a glove
finger by finger, prepared for the coming farce.

Slow as the liner she came up the stone-flagged walk
in her black church dress—a touch of the widow there—
then paused at the morning-glory to wrench a stalk

head-down, stripping its yellow petals tear by tear.
My bloody allamandas! Maud swore. And, naturally,
being you, you want me to leave the verandah,

or maybe I'll ask you up for a spot of tea.
Oh Mother of God, another allamanda!
She'll wreck the blooming garden if I don't come down.

She had timed it well. A little intimacy
between us girls. She'd seen the Land Rover in town
no doubt, but not this time, Miss Helen, *non merci*.

We aren't having any confession together;
then hated herself for her rage. Those lissome calves,
that waist swayed like a palm was her island's weather,

its clouded impulses of doing things by halves,
lowering her voice to match its muttering waves,
the deep sigh of night that came from its starlit leaves.

The cackle of her infuriating laughter
when she joked with the gardener from the kitchen,
but when Maud came to the kitchen to quiet her,

she would suck her teeth and tilt that arrogant chin
and mutter something behind her back in patois,
and when Maud asked her what, she'd smile: "Ma'am, is noffing."

Maud walked down the steps to the flagged path from the shade
of the stone porch, and Helen was starting to walk
towards her, then stopped and turned. "Morning," Helen said.

Morning. No "Madam." No "Good." All in a day's work.
Maud stopped. In midstream the liner now hovered
over Helen's tautly brushed hair. Maud nodded

as amiably as she could, but with one palm covered
over an excessive squint.
                         "So, how are you, Helen?"
"I dere, Madam."
                    At last. You dere. Of course you dare,

come back looking for work after ruining two men,
after trying on my wardrobe, after driving Hector
crazy with a cutlass, you dare come, that what you mean?

"We've no work, Helen."
                         "Is not work I looking for."
Pride edged that voice; she'd honed her arrogance
on Maud's nerves when she worked here, but there was sorrow

in the old rudeness. Helen tore the stalk in her hands.
"What I come for this morning is see if you can borrow
me five dollars. I pregnant. I will pay you next week."

Maud went as purple as one of her orchids. "I see.
How'll you pay me back, Helen, if you're out of work?
It's none of my business, but what happened to Achille?

Hector not working?"
                      "I am vexed with both of them, *oui*."
What was it in men that made such beauty evil?
She was as beautiful as a liner, but like it, she

124

changed her course, she turned her back on her friends.
"I'll fetch my purse," Maud said. Helen turned her back
and stared out to sea. This is how all beauty ends.

When Maud came with the money, she was down the track
with the arrogant sway of that hip, stern high in the line
of the turned liner. Maud stood, enraged, in the sun.

Then she picked up the flowers Helen had wrenched from the vine.
The allamandas lasted three days. Their trumpets would bend
and their glory pass. But she'd last forever, Helen.

Chapter XXIV

I

From his heart's depth he knew she was never coming
back, as he followed the skipping of a sea-swift
over the waves' changing hills, as if the humming

horizon-bow had made Africa the target
of its tiny arrow. When he saw the swift flail
and vanish in a trough he knew he'd lost Helen.

The mate was cleaning the bilge with the rusted pail
when the swift reappeared like a sunlit omen,
widening the joy that had vanished from his work.

Sunlight entered his hands, they gave that skillful twist
that angled the blade for the next stroke. Half-awake
from last night's blocko, the mate waveringly pissed

over the side, keeping his staggering balance.
"Fish go get drunk." Achille grinned. The mate cupped his hands
in the sea and lathered his head. "All right. Work start!"

He fitted the trawling rods. Achille felt the rim
of the brimming morning being brought like a gift
by the handles of the headland. He was at home.

This was his garden. God bless the speed of the swift,
God bless the wet head of the mate sparkling with foam,
and his heart trembled with enormous tenderness

for the purple-blue water and the wilting shore
tight and thin as a fishline, and the hill's blue smoke,
his muscles bulging like porpoises from each oar,

but the wrists wrenched deftly after the lifted stroke,
mesmerizing him with their incantatory
metre. The swift made a semicircular turn

over the hills, then, like a feathery lure, she
bobbed over the wake, the same distance from the stern.
He felt she was guiding and not following them

ever since she'd leapt from the blossoms of the froth
hooked to his heart, as if her one, arrowing aim
was his happiness and that was blessing enough.

Steadily she kept her distance. He said the name
that he knew her by—*l'hirondelle des Antilles*,
the tag on Maud's quilt. The mate jigged the bamboo rods

from which the baits trawled. Then it frightened Achille
that this was no swallow but the bait of the gods,
that she had seen the god's body torn from its hill.

The horned island sank. This meant they were far out,
perhaps twenty miles, over the unmarked fathoms
where the midshipman watched the frigate come about,

where no anchor has enough rope and no plummet plumbs.
His cold heart was heaving in the ancestral swell
of the ocean that had widened around the last

point where the Trades bent the almonds like a candle-
flame. He stood as the swift suddenly shot past
the hull, so closely that he thought he heard a cry

from the small parted beak, and he saw the whole world
globed in the passing sorrow of her sleepless eye.
The mate never saw her. He watched as Achille furled

both oars into one oar and laid them parallel
in the grave of *In God We Troust*, like man and wife,
like grandmother and grandfather with ritual

solicitude, then stood balancing with a knife
as firm as a gommier rooted in its own ground.
"You okay?" he said, speaking to the swaying mast.

And these were the noble and lugubrious names
under the rocking shadow of *In God We Troust*:
Habal, swept in a gale overboard; Winston James,

commonly know as *"Toujours Sou"* or "Always Soused,"
whose body disappeared, some claimed in a vapour
of white rum or l'absinthe; Herald Chastenet, plaiter

of lobster-pots, whose alias was "Fourmi Rouge,"
i.e., "Red Ant," who was terrified of water
but launched a skiff one sunrise with white-rum courage

to conquer his fear. Some fishermen could not swim.
Dorcas Henry could not, but they learnt this later
searching the pronged rocks for whelks, where they found him,

for some reason clutching a starfish. There were others
whom Achille had heard of, mainly through Philoctete,
and, of course, the nameless bones of all his brothers

drowned in the crossing, plus a Midshipman Plunkett.
He stood like a mast amidships, remembering them,
in the lace wreaths of the Caribbean anthem.

Achille looked up at the sun, it was vertical
as an anchor-rope. Its ring ironed his hot skull
like a flat iron, singeing his cap with its smell.

No action but stasis. He is riding the swell
of the line now. He lets the angling oars idle
in their wooden oarlocks. He sprinkles the scorched sail

stitched from old flour sacks and tied round the middle
with seawater from the calabash to keep it supple,
scooping with one hand over the rocking gunwale

with the beat of habit, a hand soaked in its skill,
or the stitches could split the seams, and the ply
of its knots rot from this heat. Then, as Achille

sprinkles the flour sack, he watches it dry rapidly
in a sun like a hot iron flattening his skull,
and staggers with the calabash. The tied bundle

huddles like a corpse. *Oui, Bon Dieu!* I go hurl
it overside. Out of the depths of his ritual
baptism something was rising, some white memory

of a midshipman coming up close to the hull,
a white turning body, and this water go fill
with them, turning tied canvases, not sharks, but all

corpses wrapped like the sail, and ice-sweating Achille
in the stasis of his sunstroke looked as each swell
disgorged them, in tens, in hundreds, and his soul

sickened and was ill. His jaw slackened. A gull
screeched whirling backwards, and it was the tribal
sorrow that Philoctete could not drown in alcohol.

It was not forgetful as the sea-mist or the crash
of breakers on the crisp beaches of Senegal
or the Guinea coast. He reached for the calabash

and poured it streaming over his boiling skull,
then sat back and tried to settle the wash
of bilge in his stomach. Then he began to pull

at the knots in the sail. Meanwhile, that fool
his mate went on quietly setting the fishpot.
Time is the metre, memory the only plot.

His shoulders are knobs of ebony. The back muscles
can bulge like porpoises leaping out of this line
from the gorge of our memory. His hard fists enclose

its mossed rope as bearded as a love-vine
or a blind old man, tight as a shark's jaws,
wrenching the weight, then loosening it again

as the line saws his palms' sealed calluses,
the logwood thighs anchor against the fast drain
of the trough, and here is my tamer of horses,

our only inheritance that elemental noise
of the windward, unbroken breakers, Ithaca's
or Africa's, all joining the ocean's voice,

because this is the Atlantic now, this great design
of the triangular trade. Achille saw the ghost
of his father's face shoot up at the end of the line.

Achille stared in pious horror at the bound canvas
and could not look away, or loosen its burial knots.
Then, for the first time, he asked himself who he was.

He was lured by the swift the way trolling water
mesmerizes a fisherman who stares at the
fake metal fish as the lace troughs widen and close.

III

Outrunner of flying fish, under the geometry
of the hidden stars, her wire flashed and faded
taut as a catch, this mite of the sky-touching sea

towing a pirogue a thousand times her own weight
with a hummingbird's electric wings, this engine
that shot ahead of each question like an answer,

once Achille had questioned his name and its origin.
She touched both worlds with her rainbow, this frail dancer
leaping the breakers, this dart of the meridian.

She could loop the stars with a fishline, she tired
porpoises, she circled epochs with her outstretched span;
she gave a straight answer when one was required,

she skipped the dolphin's question, she stirred every spine
of a sea-egg tickling your palm rank with the sea;
she shut the ducts of a starfish, she was the mind-

messenger, and her speed outdarted Memory.
She was the swift that he had seen in the cedars
in the foam of clouds, when she had shot across

the blue ridges of the waves, to a god's orders,
and he, at the beck of her beak, watched the bird hum
the whipping Atlantic, and felt he was headed home.

Where whales burst into flower and sails turn back
from a tiring horizon, she shot with curled feet
close to her wet belly, round-eyed, her ruddering beak

towing *In God We Troust* so fast that he felt his feet
drumming on the ridged keel-board, its shearing motion
whirred by the swift's flywheel into open ocean.

BOOK THREE

Chapter XXV

I

Mangroves, their ankles in water, walked with the canoe.
The swift, racing its browner shadow, screeched, then veered
into a dark inlet. It was the last sound Achille knew

from the other world. He feathered the paddle, steered
away from the groping mangroves, whose muddy shelves
slipped warted crocodiles, slitting the pods of their eyes;

then the horned river-horses rolling over themselves
could capsize the keel. It was like the African movies
he had yelped at in childhood. The endless river unreeled

those images that flickered into real mirages:
naked mangroves walking beside him, knotted logs
wriggling into the water, the wet, yawning boulders

of oven-mouthed hippopotami. A skeletal warrior
stood up straight in the stern and guided his shoulders,
clamped his neck in cold iron, and altered the oar.

Achille wanted to scream, he wanted the brown water
to harden into a road, but the river widened ahead
and closed behind him. He heard screeching laughter

in a swaying tree, as monkeys swung from the rafter
of their tree-house, and the bared sound rotted the sky
like their teeth. For hours the river gave the same show

for nothing, the canoe's mouth muttered its lie.
The deepest terror was the mud. The mud with no shadow
like the clear sand. Then the river coiled into a bend.

He saw the first signs of men, tall sapling fishing-stakes;
he came into his own beginning and his end,
for the swiftness of a second is all that memory takes.

Now the strange, inimical river surrenders its stealth
to the sunlight. And a light inside him wakes,
skipping centuries, ocean and river, and Time itself.

And God said to Achille, "Look, I giving you permission
to come home. Is I send the sea-swift as a pilot,
the swift whose wings is the sign of my crucifixion.

And thou shalt have no God should in case you forgot
my commandments." And Achille felt the homesick shame
and pain of his Africa. His heart and his bare head

were bursting as he tried to remember the name
of the river- and the tree-god in which he steered,
whose hollow body carried him to the settlement ahead.

He remembered this sunburnt river with its spindly
stakes and the peaked huts platformed above the spindles
where thin, naked figures as he rowed past looked unkindly

or kindly in their silence. The silence an old fence kindles
in a boy's heart. They walked with his homecoming
canoe past bonfires in a scorched clearing near the edge

of the soft-lipped shallows whose noise hurt his drumming
heart as the pirogue slid its raw, painted wedge
towards the crazed sticks of a vine-fastened pier.

The river was sloughing its old skin like a snake
in wrinkling sunshine; the sun resumed its empire
over this branch of the Congo; the prow found its stake

in the river and nuzzled it the way that a piglet
finds its favourite dug in the sweet-grunting sow,
and now each cheek ran with its own clear rivulet

of tears, as Achille, weeping, fastened the bow
of the dugout, wiped his eyes with one dry palm,
and felt a hard hand help him up the shaking pier.

Half of me was with him. One half with the midshipman
by a Dutch canal. But now, neither was happier
or unhappier than the other. An old man put an arm

around Achille, and the crowd, chattering, followed both.
They touched his trousers, his undershirt, their hands
scrabbling the texture, as a kitten does with cloth,

till they stood before an open hut. The sun stands
with expectant silence. The river stops talking,
the way silence sometimes suddenly turns off a market.

The wind squatted low in the grass. A man kept walking
steadily towards him, and he knew by that walk it
was himself in his father, the white teeth, the widening hands.

I I I

He sought his own features in those of their life-giver,
and saw two worlds mirrored there: the hair was surf
curling round a sea-rock, the forehead a frowning river,

as they swirled in the estuary of a bewildered love,
and Time stood between them. The only interpreter
of their lips' joined babble, the river with the foam,

and the chuckles of water under the sticks of the pier,
where the tribe stood like sticks themselves, reversed
by reflection. Then they walked up to the settlement,

and it seemed, as they chattered, everything was rehearsed
for ages before this. He could predict the intent
of his father's gestures; he was moving with the dead.

Women paused at their work, then smiled at the warrior
returning from his battle with smoke, from the kingdom
where he had been captured, they cried and were happy.

Then the fishermen sat near a large tree under whose dome
stones sat in a circle. His father said:

<blockquote>"Afo-la-be,"</blockquote>

touching his own heart.

<blockquote>"In the place you have come from</blockquote>

what do they call you?"

<blockquote>Time translates.</blockquote>

<blockquote>Tapping his chest,</blockquote>

the son answers:

<blockquote>"Achille." The tribe rustles, "Achille."</blockquote>

Then, like cedars at sunrise, the mutterings settle.

AFOLABE

Achille. What does the name mean? I have forgotten the one
that I gave you. But it was, it seems, many years ago.
What does it mean?

ACHILLE

<blockquote>Well, I too have forgotten.</blockquote>

Everything was forgotten. You also. I do not know.
The deaf sea has changed around every name that you gave
us; trees, men, we yearn for a sound that is missing.

AFOLABE

A name means something. The qualities desired in a son,
and even a girl-child; so even the shadows who called
you expected one virtue, since every name is a blessing,

since I am remembering the hope I had for you as a child.
Unless the sound means nothing. Then you would be nothing.
Did they think you were nothing in that other kingdom?

ACHILLE

I do not know what the name means. It means something,
maybe. What's the difference? In the world I come from
we accept the sounds we were given. Men, trees, water.

AFOLABE

And therefore, Achille, if I pointed and I said, There
is the name of that man, that tree, and this father,
would every sound be a shadow that crossed your ear,

without the shape of a man or a tree? What would it be?
(And just as branches sway in the dusk from their fear
of amnesia, of oblivion, the tribe began to grieve.)

ACHILLE

What would it be? I can only tell you what I believe,
or had to believe. It was prediction, and memory,
to bear myself back, to be carried here by a swift,

or the shadow of a swift making its cross on water,
with the same sign I was blessed with, with the gift
of this sound whose meaning I still do not care to know.

AFOLABE

No man loses his shadow except it is in the night,
and even then his shadow is hidden, not lost. At the glow
of sunrise, he stands on his own name in that light.

When he walks down to the river with the other fishermen
his shadow stretches in the morning, and yawns, but you,
if you're content with not knowing what our names mean,

then I am not Afolabe, your father, and you look through
my body as the light looks through a leaf. I am not here
or a shadow. And you, nameless son, are only the ghost

of a name. Why did I never miss you until you returned?
Why haven't I missed you, my son, until you were lost?
Are you the smoke from a fire that never burned?

There was no answer to this, as in life. Achille nodded,
the tears glazing his eyes, where the past was reflected
as well as the future. The white foam lowered its head.

Chapter XXVI

I

In a language as brown and leisurely as the river,
they muttered about a future Achille already knew
but which he could not reveal even to his breath-giver

or in the council of elders. But he learned to chew
in the ritual of the kola nut, drain gourds of palm-wine,
to listen to the moan of the tribe's triumphal sorrow

in a white-eyed storyteller to a balaphon's whine,
who perished in what battle, who was swift with the arrow,
who mated with a crocodile, who entered a river-horse

and lived in its belly, who was the thunder's favourite,
who the serpent-god conducted miles off his course
for some blasphemous offence and how he would pay for it

by forgetting his parents, his tribe, and his own spirit
for an albino god, and how that warrior was scarred
for innumerable moons so badly that he would disinherit

himself. And every night the seed-eyed, tree-wrinkled bard,
the crooked tree who carried the genealogical leaves
of the tribe in his cave-throated moaning,

traced the interlacing branches of their river-rooted lives
as intricately as the mangrove roots. Until morning
he sang, till the river was the only one to hear it.

Achille did not go down to the fishing stakes one dawn,
but left the hut door open, the hut he had been given
for himself and any woman he chose as his companion,

and he climbed a track of huge yams, to find that heaven
of soaring trees, that sacred circle of clear ground
where the gods assembled. He stood in the clearing

and recited the gods' names. The trees within hearing
ignored his incantation. He heard only the cool sound
of the river. He saw a tree-hole, raw in the uprooted ground.

II

Achille, among those voluble leaves, his people,
estranged from their chattering, withdrew in discontent.
He brooded on the river. The canoe at its pole,

doubled by its stillness, looked no different
from its reflection, nor the pier stakes, nor the thick
trees inverted at their riverline, but the shadow face

swayed by the ochre ripples seemed homesick
for the history ahead, as if its proper place
lay in unsettlement. So, to Achille, it appeared

they were not one reflection but separate men—
one crouching at the edge of the spindly pierhead,
one drowned under it, featureless in mien.

Even night was not the same. Some surrounding sorrow
with other stars that had no noise of waves
thickened in silence. At dawn, he heard a cock crow

in his head, and woke, not knowing where he was.
The sadness sank into him slowly that he was home—
that dawn-sadness which ghosts have for their graves,

because the future reversed itself in him.
He was his own memory, the shadow under the pier.
His nausea increased, he walked down to the cold river

with the other shadows, saying, "Make me happier,
make me forget the future." He laughed whenever
the men laughed in their language which was his

also. They entered the river, waist-deep. They spread
in a half-circle, with the looped net. There was peace
on the waveless river, but the surf roared in his head.

So loaded with his thoughts, like a net with the clear
and tasteless to him river-fish, was Achille—so dark
that the fishermen avoided him. They brewed a beer

which they fermented from a familiar bark
and got drunk on it, but the moment Achille wet
his memory with it, tears stung his eyes. The taste

of the bitter drink showed him Philoctete
standing in green seawater up to his waist,
hauling the canoe in, slowly, fist over fist.

1 4 1

He walked the ribbed sand under the flat keels of whales,
under the translucent belly of the snaking current,
the tiny shadows of tankers passed over him like snails

as he breathed water, a walking fish in its element.
He floated in stride, his own shadow over his eyes
like a grazing shark, through vast meadows of coral,

over barnacled cannons whose hulks sprouted anemones
like Philoctete's shin; he walked for three hundred years
in the silken wake like a ribbon of the galleons,

their bubbles fading like the transparent men-o'-wars
with their lilac dangling tendrils, bursting like aeons,
like phosphorous galaxies; he saw the huge cemeteries

of bone and the huge crossbows of the rusted anchors,
and groves of coral with hands as massive as trees
like calcified ferns and the greening gold ingots of bars

whose value had outlasted that of the privateers.
Then, one afternoon, the ocean lowered and clarified
its ceiling, its emerald net, and after three centuries

of walking, he thought he could hear the distant quarrel
of breaker with shore; then his head broke clear, and
his neck; then he could see his own shadow in the coral

grove, ribbed and rippling with light on the clear sand,
as his fins spread their toes, and he saw the leaf
of his own canoe far out, the life he had left behind

and the white line of surf around low Barrel of Beef
with its dead lantern. The salt glare left him blind
for a minute, then the shoreline returned in relief.

He woke to the sound of sunlight scratching at the door
of the hut, and he smelt not salt but the sluggish odour
of river. Fingers of light rethatched the roof's straw.

On the day of his feast they wore the same plantain trash
like Philoctete at Christmas. A bannered mitre
of bamboo was placed on his head, a calabash

mask, and skirts that made him both woman and fighter.
That was how they danced at home, to fifes and tambours,
the same berries round their necks and the small mirrors

flashing from their stuffed breasts. One of the warriors
mounted on stilts walked like lightning over the thatch
of the peaked village. Achille saw the same dances

that the mitred warriors did with their bamboo stick
as they scuttered around him, lifting, dipping their lances
like divining rods turning the earth to music,

the same chac-chac and ra-ra, the drumming the same,
and the chant of the seed-eyed prophet to the same
response from the blurring ankles. The same, the same.

Chapter XXVII

He could hear the same echoes made by their stone axes
in the heights over the tied sticks of the settlement,
and the echoes were prediction and memory, the crossing X's

of the sidewise strokes, but here in their element
the trees and the spirits that they uttered were
rooted, and Achille looked at the map in his hand

rivered as numerously as this, his coast. Then war
came. One day a drizzle of shafts arched and fanned
over the screaming huts, and the archers with blurred stride

ran through the kitchen gardens, trampling the yams,
and the dogs whirled, barking. Achille could not hide
or fight. He stood in their centre, with useless arms.

The raid was swift. It was done before he knew it.
Its accomplishment lay in its strategy of surprise.
It had caught the village in the flung arc of a net

with its mesh of whirling archers whose baboon cries
terrified the dogs, had stumbling mothers shrieking for
their standing children. Noise was as much its weapon.

The fishermen, hearing the cries from the ochre shore
of the river, dropped their vines, woven with grass
and reeds, and ran as if they themselves were a race

of river sprats, entered the mouth of the ambush
where a new brace of archers rose, and another brace
erect from the reeds, suddenly grown from the bush.

The raid was profitable. It yielded fifteen slaves
to the slavers waiting up the coast. The brown river
in the silence rippled under the settlement in waves

of forgetful light. Swifts crossbowed across it, a quiver
of arrowheads. Achille walked in the dusty street
of the barren village. The doors were like open graves.

I I

Achille climbed a ridge. He counted the chain of men
linked by their wrists with vines; he watched until
the line was a line of ants. He let out a soft moan

as the last ant disappeared. Then he went downhill.
He paused at the thorn barrier surrounding the village.
Then he entered it. Dust hazed the path. A mongrel

and a child sat in the street, the child with a clay
bowl in its hands, squatting in the dust. The fanged growl
backed away from his shadow. Achille turned away

down another street. Then another, to more and more
silence. There were arrow shafts lying in the dust
around the thatched houses. He creaked open a door.

Achille saw Seven Seas foaming with grief. He must
be deaf as well as blind, Achille thought. The head
never turned but it widened its mouth to the river,

the same list of battles the river had already heard.
Achille shut the thatch door. Where were all the dead?
Where were the women? Then he returned to look for the

child and the ribbed dog. Both had disappeared.
Once, he thought he heard voices behind a thorn barrier,
when a swivel of dust rose. He went down to the pier

and saw the other dugouts nuzzling the crooked poles
and his own canoe, and nothing was strange; it
was sharply familiar. They'd vanished into their souls.

He foresaw their future. He knew nothing could change it.
The tinkle from coins of the river, the tinkle of irons.
The son's grief was the father's, the father's his son's.

He climbed down to the steps of the pier and undid
the green mossed liana and towed it towards him
gently. The canoe came like a dog. And then Achille died

again. Thinking of the ants arriving at the sea's rim,
or climbing the pyramids of coal and entering inside
the dark hold, far from this river and the griot's hymn.

III

He walked slowly back to the peaked hut where the council
was always held, where, until the last embers of starlight,
the men sat with the griot, drinking from the bark bowl.

The griot crouched there. Warm ashes made his skull white
over eyes sore as embers, over a skin charred as coal,
the core of his toothless mouth, groaning to the firelight,

was like a felled cedar's whose sorrow surrounds its bole.
One hand clawed the pile of ashes, the other fist thudded on
the drum of his chest, the ribs were like a caved-in canoe

that rots for years under the changing leaves of an almond,
while the boys who played war in it become grown men who
work, marry, and die, until their own sons in turn

rock the rotted hulk, or race in it, pretending to row,
as Achille had done in the manchineel grove as a boy.
Seven Seas was like that canoe, with the bilge of his prow

choked with old leaves, old words, by a blue, silent bay.
Achille looked round the hut. But what he looked for
was not certain. A weapon. A lance with its stone leaf,

or a shield stretched from pigskin, the mane of a warrior,
or the earth-dyes whose streakings would mask his grief
in their fury. There was one spear only. An oar.

He ran down to the pier. In the nets were their eyes
that seared through his skull; he cried his father's name
over the river. Then he swam to the opposite trees.

He cut off their circle. He hid and felt the same
mania that, in the arrows of drizzle, he felt for Hector.
He let them pass. One was laggard; with a clenched roar

he swung at the grinning laggard and the bladed oar
cleft through his skull with a sound like a calabash,
splattering his chest with brain; then the archer

thudded in his death-throes like a spear-gaffed fish
as Achille hammered and hammered him with the oar's head,
as the skull grinned up at him with skinned yellow teeth

like a baboon mating; then Achille wrenched the bow
from the locked hand, and then, sobbing with grief
at the death of a brother, he shot like the brown arrow

of the sea-swift through ferns, not shaking their leaves,
brushing webbed vines from his face, and the leaf-shade
freckled him like an ocelot, like the leopard loping,

as he hurdled the roots, raking the way clear of the net
of vines, till his palm was streaked with blood, unroping
himself from their thorns, his eyes salted with sweat,

and the one thought thudding in him was, I can deliver
all of them by hiding in a half-circle, then I could
change their whole future, even the course of the river

would flow backwards, past the mangroves. Then a cord
of thorned vine looped his tendon, encircling the heel
with its own piercing chain. He fell hard. He saw

the leaves pinned with stars. Ants crawled over Achille
as his blind eyes stared from the mud, still as the archer
he had brained, the bow beside him and the broken oar.

Chapter XXVIII

I

Now he heard the griot muttering his prophetic song
of sorrow that would be the past. It was a note, long-drawn
and endless in its winding like the brown river's tongue:

"We were the colour of shadows when we came down
with tinkling leg-irons to join the chains of the sea,
for the silver coins multiplying on the sold horizon,

and these shadows are reprinted now on the white sand
of antipodal coasts, your ashen ancestors
from the Bight of Benin, from the margin of Guinea.

There were seeds in our stomachs, in the cracking pods
of our skulls on the scorching decks, the tubers
withered in no time. We watched as the river-gods

changed from snakes into currents. When inspected,
our eyes showed dried fronds in their brown irises,
and from our curved spines, the rib-cages radiated

like fronds from a palm-branch. Then, when the dead
palms were heaved overside, the ribbed corpses
floated, riding, to the white sand they remembered,

to the Bight of Benin, to the margin of Guinea.
So, when you see burnt branches riding the swell,
trying to reclaim the surf through crooked fingers,

after a night of rough wind by some stone-white hotel,
past the bright triangular passage of the windsurfers,
remember us to the black waiter bringing the bill."

But they crossed, they survived. There is the epical splendour.
Multiply the rain's lances, multiply their ruin,
the grace born from subtraction as the hold's iron door

rolled over their eyes like pots left out in the rain,
and the bolt rammed home its echo, the way that thunder-
claps perpetuate their reverberation.

So there went the Ashanti one way, the Mandingo another,
the Ibo another, the Guinea. Now each man was a nation
in himself, without mother, father, brother.

II

The worst crime is to leave a man's hands empty.
Men are born makers, with that primal simplicity
in every maker since Adam. This is pre-history,

that itching instinct in the criss-crossed net
of their palms, its wickerwork. They could not
stay idle too long. The chained wrists couldn't forget

the carver for whom antelopes leapt, or
the bow-maker the shaft, or the armourer
his nail-studs, the shield held up to Hector

that was the hammerer's art. So the wet air
revolved in the potter's palms, in the painter's eye
the arcs of a frantic springbok bucked soundlessly,

baboons kept signing their mimetic alphabet
in case men forgot it, so out of habit
their fingers grew leaves in the foetid ground of the boat.

So now they were coals, firewood, dismembered
branches, not men. They had left their remembered
shadows to the firelight. Scratching a board

they made the signs for their fading names on the wood,
and their former shapes returned absently; each carried
the nameless freight of himself to the other world.

Then, after wreaths of seaweed, after the bitter nouns
of strange berries, coral sores, after the familiar irons
singing round their ankles, after the circling suns,

dry sand their soles knew. Sand they could recognize.
Men they knew by their hearts. They came up from the darkness
past the disinterested captains, shielding their eyes.

III

Not where russet lions snarl on leaf-blown terraces,
or where ocelots carry their freckled shadows, or wind erases
Assyria, or where drizzling arrows hit the unflinching faces

of some Thracian phalanx winding down mountain passes,
but on a palm shore, with its vines and river grasses,
and stone barracoons, on brown earth, bare as their asses.

Yet they felt the sea-wind tying them into one nation
of eyes and shadows and groans, in the one pain
that is inconsolable, the loss of one's shore

with its crooked footpath. They had wept, not for
their wives only, their fading children, but for strange,
ordinary things. This one, who was a hunter,

wept for a sapling lance whose absent heft sang
in his palm's hollow. One, a fisherman, for an ochre
river encircling his calves; one a weaver, for the straw

fishpot he had meant to repair, wilting in water.
They cried for the little thing after the big thing.
They cried for a broken gourd. It was only later

that they talked to the gods who had not been there
when they needed them. Their whole world was moving,
or a large part of the world, and what began dissolving

was the fading sound of their tribal name for the rain,
the bright sound for the sun, a hissing noun for the river,
and always the word "never," and never the word "again."

Chapter XXIX

I

At noon a ground dove hidden somewhere in the trees
whooed like a conch or a boy blowing a bottle
stuck on one note with maddening, tireless cries;

it was lower than the nightingale's full throttle
of grief, but to Helen, stripping dried sheets along
the wire in Hector's yard, the monodic moan

came from the hole in her heart. It was not the song
that twittered from the veined mesh of Agamemnon,
but the low-fingered O of an Aruac flute.

She rested the sheets down, she threw stones at the noise
in that lime-tree past the fence, and looked for the flight
of the startled dove from the branches of her nerves.

But the O's encircled her, black as the old tires
where Hector grew violets, like bubbles in soapy
water where she scrubbed the ribbed washboard so hard tears

blurred her wrist. Not Helen now, but Penelope,
in whom a single noon was as long as ten years,
because he had not come back, because they had gone

from yesterday, because the fishermen's fears
spread in the surfing trees. She watched a bleaching-stone
drying with lather, the print of wet feet fading

where she had unpinned the yellow dress from the line,
while the ground dove cooed and cooed, so sorrow-laden
in its lime-tree, that the lemon dress was her sign.

Embracing the dry sheets, Helen entered the house
where the moan could not reach her, she crammed the sheets down
in the basket. She unhooked her skirt, then the blouse,

panties and bra. She sprawled on the unmade bed, brown
and naked as God made her. The hand was not hers
that crawled like a crab, lower and lower down

into the cave of her thighs, it was not Hector's
but Achille's hand yesterday. She turns slowly round
on her stomach and comes as soon as he enters.

II

Lonely as a bachelor's plate, a full moon cleared
the suds of the clouds. Seven Seas felt the moonlight
on his hands, washing his wares. The dog appeared.

He scraped rice and fish into its enamel plate
and said, "Watch the bones, eh!"; then he smelt Philoctete
entering the yard, making sure to hook back the gate

so the dog wouldn't slide out. He said: "Nice moonlight,"
following the man's sore's smell. "No news about your friend, yet?"
he asked in English. Philoctete sat on the same

step he chose every moonlight and said in Creole:
"They say he drown." The dog chewed noisily.
                                        "His name
is what he out looking for, his name and his soul,"

Seven Seas said.
            "Where that?"
                        They both looked at the moon.
It made the yard clean, it clarified every leaf.
"Africa," the blind one said. "He go come back soon."

Philoctete nodded. What else was left to believe
but miracles? Whose vision except a blind man's,
or a blind saint's, her name as bright as the island's?

III

On that moonlit night I was snoring, cupping her side,
when she shook me off from her damp flesh with a shout
that bristled me. She yanked the chain of her bedside

lamp, as I, with ponderous head and wincing snout,
saw her hands claw her face. As I shifted closer
she flailed me away in terror and she cowered

close to the headboard, so I moved to enclose her
within my split trotters, with my curved tusks lowered,
spines prickling my hunch. "Monster!" She shuddered. "Monster!

I turned round to watch your face while you were sleeping,
and you snored, rooting a trough, and covered with flies."
By then, if monsters weep, I would have been weeping

through the half-sleep that still gummed my slitted eyes.
Her fingers were branches. I boared through their bracken
towards her breasts, and their tenderness took me in.

I felt her sobbing, then her small shoulders slacken
to her body's smile. "Oh, God, I drank too much wine
at dinner last night." Then Circe embraced her swine.

Now, running home, Achille sprung up from the seabed
like a weightless astronaut, not flexing his knees
through phosphorescent sleep; the parchment overhead

of crinkling water recorded three centuries
of the submerged archipelago, in its swell
the world above him passed through important epochs

in which treaties were shredded like surf, governments fell,
markets soared and plunged, but never once did the shocks
of power find a just horizon, from capture

in chains to long debates over manumission,
from which abolitionists soared in a rapture
of guilt. Kings lost their minds. A Jesuit mission

burned in Veracruz; fleeing the Inquisition
a Sephardic merchant, bag locked in one elbow,
crouched by a Lisbon dock, and in that position

was reborn in the New World: Lima; Curaçao.
A snow-headed Negro froze in the Pyrenees,
an ape behind bars, to Napoleon's orders,

but the dark fathoms were godless, then the waters
grew hungrier and a wave swallowed Port Royal.
Victoria revolved with her gold orb and sceptre,

Wilberforce was struck by lightning, a second Saul
at the crossroads of empire, while the spectre
breathed in the one element that had made them all

fishes and men; Darwin claimed fishes equal
in the sight of the sea. Madrasi climbed the hull
with their rolled bundles from Calcutta and Bombay,

huddling like laundry in the hold of the *Fatel
Rozack*, ninety-six days out and forty-one more away
from the Cape of Good Hope. In a great sea-battle,

before them, a midshipman was wounded and drowned.
Dawn brought a sea-drizzle. Achille, cramped from a sound
sleep, watched the lights of the morning plane as it droned.

Chapter XXX

I

He yawned and watched the lilac horns of his island
lift the horizon.
        "I know you ain't like to talk,"
the mate said, "but this morning I could use a hand.

Where your mind was whole night?"
                    "Africa."
                                    "Oh? You walk?"
The mate held up his T-shirt, mainly a red hole,
and wriggled it on. He tested the bamboo pole

that trawled the skipping lure from the fast-shearing hull
with the Trade behind them.
                    "Mackerel running," he said.
"Africa, right! You get sunstroke, chief. That is all.

You best put that damn captain-cap back on your head."
All night he had worked the rods without any sleep,
watching Achille cradled in the bow; he had read

the stars and known how far out they were and how deep
the black troughs were and how long it took them to lift,
but he owed it to his captain, who took him on

when he was stale-drunk. He had not noticed the swift.
"You know what we ketch last night? One *mako* size 'ton,' "
using the patois for kingfish, blue albacore.

"Look by your foot."
                    The kingfish, steel-blue and silver,
lay fresh at his feet, its eye like a globed window
ringing with cold, its rim the circular river

of the current that had carried him back, with the spoon
bait in its jaw, the ton was his deliverer,
now its cold eye in sunlight was blind as the moon.

A grey lens clouded the gaze of the albacore
that the mate had gaffed and clubbed. It lay there, gaping,
its blue flakes yielding the oceanic colour

of the steel-cold depth from which it had shot, leaping,
stronger than a stallion's neck tugging its stake,
sounding, then bursting its trough, yawning at the lure

of a fishhook moon that was reeled in at daybreak
round the horizon's wrist. Tired of slapping water,
the tail's wedge had drifted into docility.

Achille had slept through the fight. Cradled at the bow
like a foetus, like a sea-horse, his memory
dimmed in the sun with the scales of the albacore.

"Look, land!" the mate said. Achille altered the rudder
to keep sideways in the deep troughs without riding
the crests, then he looked up at an old man-o'-war

tracing the herring-gulls with that endless gliding
that made it the sea-king.
                "Them stupid gulls does fish
for him every morning. He himself don't catch none,

white slaves for a black king."
                   "When?" the mate said. "You wish.
"Look him dropping." Achille pointed. "Look at that son-
of-a-bitch stealing his fish for the whole fucking week!"

A herring-gull climbed with silver bent in its beak
and the black magnificent frigate met the gull
halfway with the tribute; the gull dropped the mackerel

but the frigate-bird caught it before it could break
the water and soared.
              "The black bugger beautiful,
though!" The mate nodded, and Achille felt the phrase lift

his heart as high as the bird whose wings wrote the word
"Afolabe," in the letters of the sea-swift.
"The king going home," he said as he and the mate

watched the frigate steer into that immensity
of seraphic space whose cumuli were a gate
dividing for a monarch entering his city.

II

Like parchment charts at whose corners four winged heads spout
jets of curled, favouring gusts, their cheeks like cornets
till the sails belly as the hull goes hard about

through seas as scrolled as dragons in ornate knots,
so strong gusts favoured the sail, until he could shout
from happiness, except that the mate would have heard.

This was the shout on which each odyssey pivots,
that silent cry for a reef, or familiar bird,
not the outcry of battle, not the tangled plots

of a fishnet, but when a wave rhymes with one's grave,
a canoe with a coffin, once that parallel
is crossed, and cancels the line of master and slave.

Then an uplifted oar is stronger than marble
Caesar's arresting palm, and a swift outrigger
fleeter than his galleys in its skittering bliss.

And I'm homing with him, Homeros, my nigger,
my captain, his breastplates bursting with happiness!
Let the dolphins like outriders escort him now

past Barrel of Beef, because he can see the white
balconies of the hotel dipping with the bow,
and, under his heel, the albacore's silver weight.

III

And this was the hymn that Achille could not utter:
"*Merci, Bon Dieu, pour la mer-a, merci la Vierge*"—
"Thank God for the sea who is His Virgin Mother";

"*Qui ba moin force moin*"— "Who gave me the privilege
of working for Him. Every bird is my brother";
"*Toutes gibiers c'est frères moin', pis n'homme ni pour travail*"—

"Because man must work like the birds until he die."
He could see the heightening piles of the jetty
in front of the village hung with old tires, the mate

standing in his torn red shirt, the anchor ready,
then the conch-shell blowing and blowing its low note
like a ground dove's. And way up, in his yam garden,

Philoctete planting green yam shoots heard the moaning sea,
and crossed his bare, caving chest, and asked God pardon
for his doubt. In the sharp shade of the pharmacy

Seven Seas heard it; he heard it before the dog
thudded its tail on the box and the fishermen
ran down the hot street to pull the tired pirogue.

Achille let the mate wave back. Then he saw Helen.
But he said nothing. He sculled with a single oar.
He watched her leave. The mate hoisted the albacore.

Chapter XXXI

A remorseful Saturday strolled through the village,
down littered pavements, the speakers gone from the street
whose empty shadows contradicted the mirage

of last night's blockorama, but the systems' beat
thudded in Achille's head that replayed the echo,
as he washed the canoe, of a Marley reggae—

"Buffalo soldier." Thud. "Heart of America."
Thud-thud. Mop and pail. He could not rub it away.
Between the soft thud of surf the bass beat wider,

backing his work up with its monodic phrasing.
He saw the smoky buffalo, a black rider
under a sweating hat, his slitted eyes grazing

with the herds that drifted like smoke under low hills,
the wild Indian tents, the sky's blue screen, and on it,
the black soldier turned his face, and it was Achille's.

Then, pennons in reggae-motion, a white bonnet
in waves of heat like a sea-horse, leading them in
their last wide charge, the soft hooves pounding in his skull,

Red Indians bouncing to a West Indian rhythm,
to the cantering beat which, as he swayed, the scull
of the lance-like oar kept up like a metronome,

as, fist by fist, from the bow he pulled up anchor,
he saw, like palms on a ridge, the Red Indians come
with blurred hooves drumming to the music's sweet anger,

while his own horse neighed and stamped, smelling a battle
in its own sweat. Achille eased the long Winchester
out of its fringed case. This was the oar. His saddle

the heaving plank at the stern, a wave's crest was the
white eagle bonnet; then slowly he fired the oar
and a palm-tree crumpled; then to repeated cracks

from the rifle, more savages, until the shore
was littered with palm spears, bodies: like Aruacs
falling to the muskets of the Conquistador.

II

Seven Seas asked him to rake the leaves in his yard.
The pomme-Arac shed so many the rusted drum
filled quickly, and more were falling as he carried

each pile. Through the teeth of the rake Achille heard them
talk a dead language. He would clean up this whole place.
He cutlassed the banana trash. He gripped a frond

of the rusting coconut, swivelling its base
till it gave, then he dumped the rubbish in a mound
round the smoking drum. The black dog did dog-dances

around him, yapping, crouching, entangling his heel.
Meanwhile, the bonfire rose with crackling branches.
Seven Seas, on his box, called the dog from Achille.

He wanted to ask Seven Seas where trees got names,
watching the ribbed branches blacken with the same stare
of the blind man at the leaves of the leaping flames,

and why our life's spark is exceeded by a star.
But the light of a star is dead and maybe our
light was the same. Then Achille saw the iguana

in the leaves of the pomme-Arac branches and fear
froze him at the same time it fuelled the banner
of the climbing flame. Then the ridged beast disappeared.

He stepped back from the pomme-Arac's shade on the grass
diagrammed like the lizard. Then, as if he heard
his thought, Seven Seas said: "Aruac mean the race

that burning there like the leaves and pomme is the word
in patois for 'apple.' This used to be their place."
Maybe he'd heard the iguana with his dog's ears,

because the dog was barking around the trunk's base.
He had never heard the dog's name either. It was
one of those Saturdays that contain centuries,

when the strata of history layered underheel,
which earth sometimes flashes with its mineral signs,
can lie in a quartz shard. Gradually, Achille

found History that morning. Near the hedge, the tines
of the rake in the dead leaves grated on some stone,
so he crouched to uproot the obstruction. He saw

deep marks in the rock that froze his fingers to bone.
The features incised there glared back at his horror
from its disturbed grave. A face that a child will draw:

blank circles for eyes, a straight line down for the nose,
a slit for a mouth, but the expression angrier
as Achille's palm brushed off centuries of repose.

A thousand archaeologists started screaming
as Achille wrenched out the totem, then hurled it far
over the oleander hedge. It lay dreaming

on one cheek in the spear-grass, but that act of fear
multiplied the lances on his scalp. Stone-faced souls
peered with their lizard eyes through the pomme-Arac tree,

then turned from their bonfire. Instantly, like moles
or mole crickets in the shadow of History,
the artifacts burrowed deeper into their holes.

III

A beach burns their memory. Copper almond leaves
cracking like Caribs in a pepper smoke, the blue
entering God's eye and nothing raked from their lives

except one elegy from Aruac to Sioux,
the shadow of a frond's bonnet riding white sand,
while Seven Seas tried to tell Achille the answer

to certain names. The cane's question shook in his hand
while the pomme-Arac leaves burned. He said he was once
a Ghost Dancer like that smoke. He described the snow

to Achille. He named the impossible mountains
that he had seen when he lived among the Indians.
Sybils sweep the sand of our archipelago.

Chapter XXXII

She floated so lightly! One hand, frail as a swift,
gripping the verandah. The cotton halo fanned
from her shrunken crown, and I felt that I could lift

that fledgling, my mother, in the cup of my hand
and settle her somewhere else: away from the aged
women rubbing rosaries in the Marian Home,

but I was resigned like them. I no longer raged
at the humiliations of time. Her turn had come
to be bent by its weight, its indifferent process

that drummed in wrist and shank. Time was that fearful friend
they talked to, who sat beside them in empty chairs,
as deaf as they were; who sometimes simply listened.

They were all withdrawn. They'd entered a dimension
where every thought was weightless, every form clouded
by its ephemeral halo. Time's intention

rather than death was what baffled them; in the deed
of dying there was terror, but what did time mean,
after some friend stopped talking and around her bed

they opened the panels of an unfolding screen?
The frail hair grew lovelier on my mother's head,
but when my arm rested on her hollow shoulder

it staggered slightly from the solicitous weight.
I was both father and son. I was as old as her
exhausted prayer, as her wisps of memory floated

with a vague patience, telling her body: "Wait,"
when all that brightness had withered like memory's flower,
like the allamanda's bells and the pale lilac

bougainvillea vines that had covered our gabled house.
They, like her natural memory, would not come back.
Her days were dim as dusk. There were no more hours.

From her cupped sleep, she wavered with recognition.
I would bring my face closer to hers and catch the
scent of her age.
                    "Who am I? Mama, I'm your son."

"My son." She nodded.
                        "You have two, and a daughter.
And a lot of grandchildren," I shouted. "A lot to
remember."
              "A lot." She nodded, as she fought her

memory. "Sometimes I ask myself who I am."
We looked at the hills together, at roofs that I knew
in childhood. "Their names are Derek, Roddy, and Pam."

"I have to go back to the States again."
                                          "Well, we
can't be together all the time," she said, "I know."
"There is too much absence," I said. Then a blessed

lucidity broke through a cloud. She smiled. "I know
who you are. You are my son."
                              "Warwick's son," she said.
"Nature's gentleman." His vine-leaves haloed her now.

166

I left her on the verandah with her white hair,
to buckets clanging in the African twilight
where two girls at the standpipe collected water,

and children with bat-like cries seemed trapped behind bright
galvanized fences, and down the thickening road
as bulbs came on behind curtains, the shadows crossed

me, signing their black language. I felt transported,
past shops smelling of cod to a place I had lost
in the open book of the street, and could not find.

It was another country, whose excitable
gestures I knew but could not connect with my mind,
like my mother's amnesia; untranslatable

answers accompanied these actual spirits
who had forgotten me as much as I, too, had
forgotten a continent in the narrow streets.

Now, in night's unsettling noises, what I heard
enclosed my skin with an older darkness. I stood
in a village whose fires flickered in my head

with tongues of a speech I no longer understood,
but where my flesh did not need to be translated;
then I heard patois again, as my ears unclogged.

The bay was black in starlight. The reek of the beach
was rimmed with a white noise. The beam of the lighthouse
revolved over trees and skipped what it couldn't reach.

The fronds were threshing over the lit bungalows,
and a breaker arched with a sound like tearing cloth
ripped down the stitched seam, a sound Mama made sewing

when, in disgust, she'd rip the stitches with her mouth.
As I closed the door I felt the surf-noise going
far out back to sea, from each window, one by one,

and yet, inside the rooms was this haze of motion,
above the taut sheet still fragrant from the iron,
and I watched, enlarged by the lamp, a stuttering moth.

III

The moth's swift shadow rippled on an emerald
lagoon that clearly showed the submerged geography
of the reef's lilac shelf, where a lateen sail held

for Gros Îlet village like a hooked butterfly
on its flowering branch: a canoe, nearing the island.
Soundless, enormous breakers foamed across the pane,

then broke into blinding glare. Achille raised his hand
from the drumming rudder, then watched our minnow plane
melt into cloud-coral over the horned island.

BOOK FOUR

Chapter XXXIII

I

With the stunned summer going, with the barrel-organ
oaks, the fiddles of gnats, with the surrendering groan
of a carousel by Long Island Sound, the lake with a moon

adrift there in daylight like an unstrung balloon,
with the cold in your palm like a statue's on
your girlfriend's knee, from the wooden croak of a loon

from the summer-theatre, the picnic tents of New London,
by the tidal rock-pools, from the broiled prawn
of faces in salad landscapes, to the folding accordion

of fin-de-siècle wave swells, the circuses came down
along the coast of my new empire; the carousels stiffen,
and pegs are pulled from grass that is going brown

in the early cold. They live by an unceasing
self-deceit in an eternal republic, by the vernal sin
in the blue distance, as summer widens its increasing

pardon. Clouds unbutton their bodices,
and butterflies sail in their yellow odysseys,
and shadows everywhere wear the same size.

But the horizon is closer as the awnings fold
and the flags and guywires are pulled down, and the field
is left to its broad scar. Now the bleachers are too cold

except for stubborn lovers who think that the night
will say its stars for the first time. It is late
for us to measure our footfall. And the dark slate

Sound that is scratched with chalk lines, the lighthouses
squinting in the fog, the slowly buttoned blouses
make us walk slowly, Mayakovsky's clouds in trousers.

From the provincial edge of an atlas, from the hem
of a frayed empire, a man stops. Not for another anthem
trembling over the water—he has learnt three of them—

but for that faint sidereal drone interrupted by the air
gusting over black water, or so that he can hear
the surf in the pores of wet sand wince and pucker.

II

Back in a Brookline of brick and leaf-shaded lanes
I lived like a Japanese soldier in World War
II, on white rice and spare ribs, and, just for a change,

spare ribs and white rice, until the Chinese waiter
setting my corner-table muttered my order,
halfheartedly flashing the bedragonned menu.

Like a Jap soldier on his Pacific island
who prefers solitude to the hope of rescue,
I could blend with the decor of its bamboo grove

and read my paper in peace. I knew they all knew
about my abandonment in the war of love:
the busboys, the couples, their eyes turned from the smell

of failure, while my own eyes had turned Japanese
looking for a letter, for its rescuing sail,
till I grew tired, like wounded Philoctetes,

the hermit who did not know the war was over,
or refused to believe it. The late summer light
squared the carpet, moved from the floor to the sofa,

moved from the sofa, which turned to a hill at night.
But even at night the heat stayed in the concrete
pavements while the fan whirred its steel blades like a palm's,

as I brushed imaginary sand off from my feet,
turned off the light, and pillowed her waist with my arms,
then tossed on my back. The fan turned, rustling the sheet.

I reached from my raft and reconnected the phone.
In its clicking oarlocks, it idled, my one oar.
But castaways make friends with the sea; living alone

they learn to survive on fistfuls of rainwater
and windfall sardines. But a house which is unblest
by familiar voices, startled by the clatter

of cutlery in a sink with absence for its guest,
as it drifts, its rooms intact, in doldrum summer,
is less a mystery than the *Marie Celeste*.

Hot concrete pavements, storefronts with watery glass,
in supermarkets her back steering a basket,
same hair, same shoulders, same compact, cynical ass

rounding the aisle, afraid of things I might ask it.
Her wrist yanking the trolley cord and the trolley
gliding with its bell to a stop, as she gets off

to her fixed appointments. Down some chic side-alley
with its bakery and boutiques, the dead-end of love—
all taken in stride as the car picks up slowly

and passes her confident hair, gathering speed,
past faces frowning at the sunlight as she,
walking backwards with the crowd, begins to recede

with shapes on a wharf; or her elbow in the shade
of a florist's awning, that, as I grew closer
to the sprinkled shelves, disappeared like a lizard,

while I stood there, in the aisles of Vallombrosa,
drugged by the perfume of flowers I didn't need.
Then, back to the sunstruck pavement, where passers-by

avoided my dewy gaze with a cautious nod,
when they were the busy, transparent ones, not I.
I had nowhere to go but home. Yet I was lost.

Like them I could jiggle keys in purse or pocket.
Like them I fiddled with the door, hoping a ghost
would rise from her chair and help me to unlock it.

House of umbrage, house of fear,
house of multiplying air

House of memories that grow
like shadows out of Allan Poe

House where marriages go bust,
house of telephone and lust

House of caves, behind whose door
a wave is crouching with its roar

House of toothbrush, house of sin,
of branches scratching, "Let me in!"

House whose rooms echo with rain,
of wrinkled clouds with Onan's stain

House that creaks, age fifty-seven,
wooden earth and plaster heaven

House of channelled CableVision
whose dragonned carpets sneer derision

Unlucky house that I uncurse
by rites of genuflecting verse

House I unhouse, house that can harden
as cold as stones in the lost garden

House where I look down the scorched street
but feel its ice ascend my feet

I do not live in you, I bear
my house inside me, everywhere

until your winters grow more kind
by the dancing firelight of mind

where knobs of brass do not exist,
whose doors dissolve with tenderness

House that lets in, at last, those fears
that are its guests, to sit on chairs

feasts on their human faces, and
takes pity simply by the hand

shows her her room, and feels the hum
of wood and brick becoming home.

Chapter XXXIV

I

The Crow horseman pointed his lance at the contrail
high over the Dakotas, over Colorado's
palomino mountains; shapes so edged with detail

I mistook them for lakes. Under the crumbling floes
of a gliding Arctic were dams large as our cities,
and the icy contrails scratched on the Plexiglas

hung like white comets left by their seraphic skis.
Clouds whitened the Crow horseman and I let him pass
into the page, and I saw the white waggons move

across it, with printed ruts, then the railroad track
and the arrowing interstate, as a lost love
narrowed from epic to epigram. Our contracts

were torn like the clouds, like treaties with the Indians,
but with mutual treachery. Through the window,
the breakers burst like the spray on Pacific pines,

and Manifest Destiny was behind me now.
My face frozen in the ice-cream paradiso
of the American dream, like the Sioux in the snow.

II

The wandering smoke below me was like Achille's
hallucination. Lances, the shattering silver
of cavalry fording a stream, as oxen-wheels

grooved the Republic towards her. A spike hammered
into the heart of their country as the Sioux looked on.
The spike for the Union Pacific had entered

my heart without cheers for her far gentler weapon.
I could not believe it was over any more
than they did. Their stunned, anachronistic faces

moved through the crowd, or stood, with the same expression
that I saw in my own when I looked through the glass,
for a land that was lost, a woman who was gone.

The elegies of summer sighed in the marram,
to bending Virgilian reeds. Languid meadows
raised their natural fly-screens around the Parkin farm.

Larks arrowed from the goldenrod into soft doors
of enclosing thunderheads, and the rattled maize
threshed like breaking surf to Catherine Weldon's ears.

Ripe grain alchemized the pheasant, the pelt of mice
nibbling the stalks was unctuous as the beaver's,
but the sky was scribbled with the prophetic cries

of multiplying hawks. The grass by the rivers
shone silvery green whenever its nub of felt
was chafed between the thumb and finger of the wind;

rainbow trout leapt arching into canoes and filled
their bark bodies while a clear wake chuckled behind
the gliding hunter. An immensity of peace

across which the thunderheads rumbled like waggons,
to which the hawk held the rights, a rolling excess
from knoll and pasture concealed the wound of her son's

death from a rusty nail. It returned the image
when the goldenrod quivered, from a golden past:
Flushed wings. A shot. Her husband hoisting a partridge,

still flapping, towards her. That summer did not last,
but time wasn't treacherous. What would not remain
was not only the season but the tribes themselves,

as Indian summer raced the cloud-galloping plain,
when their dust would blow like maize from the furrowed shelves,
which the hawks prophesied to mice cowering in grain.

Chapter XXXV

I

"Somewhere over there," said my guide, "the Trail of Tears
started." I leant towards the crystalline creek. Pines
shaded it. Then I made myself hear the water's

language around the rocks in its clear-running lines
and its small shelving falls with their eddies, "Choctaws,"
"Creeks," "Choctaws," and I thought of the Greek revival

carried past the names of towns with columned porches,
and how Greek it was, the necessary evil
of slavery, in the catalogue of Georgia's

marble past, the Jeffersonian ideal in
plantations with its Hectors and Achilleses,
its foam in the dogwood's spray, past towns named Helen,

Athens, Sparta, Troy. The slave shacks, the rolling peace
of the wave-rolling meadows, oak, pine, and pecan,
and a creek like this one. From the window I saw

the bundles of women moving in ragged bands
like those on the wharf, headed for Oklahoma;
then I saw Seven Seas, a rattle in his hands.

A huge thunderhead was unclenching its bruised fist
over the county. Shadows escaped through the pines
and the pecan groves and hounds were closing in fast

deep into Georgia, where history happens
to be the baying echoes of brutality,
and terror in the oaks along red country roads,

or the gibbet branches of a silk-cotton tree
from which Afolabes hung like bats. Hooded clouds
guarded the town squares with their calendar churches,

whose white, peaked belfries asserted that pastoral
of brooks with leisurely accents. On their verges,
like islands reflected on windscreens, Negro shacks

moved like a running wound, like the rusty anchor
that scabbed Philoctete's shin, I imagined the backs
moving through the foam of pods, one arm for an oar,

one for the gunny sack. Brown streams tinkled in chains.
Bridges arched their spines. Led into their green pasture,
horses sagely grazed or galloped the plantations.

II

"Life is so fragile. It trembles like the aspens.
All its shadows are seasonal, including pain.
In drizzling dusk the rain enters the lindens

with its white lances, then lindens enclose the rain.
So that day isn't far when they will say, 'Indians
bowed under those branches, which tribe is not certain.'

Nor am I certain I lived. I breathed what the farm
exhaled. Its soils, its seasons. The swayed goldenrod,
the corn where summer hid me, pollen on my arm,

sweat tickling my armpits. The Plains were fierce as God
and wide as His mind. I enjoyed diminishing,
I exalted in insignificance after

the alleys of Boston, in the unfinishing
chores of the farm, alone. Once, from the barn's rafter
a swift or a swallow shot out, taking with it

my son's brown, whirring soul, and I knew that its aim
was heaven. More and more we learn to do without
those we still love. With my father it was the same.

The bounty of God pursued me over the Plains
of the Dakotas, the pheasants, the quick-volleyed
arrows of finches; smoke bound me to the Indians

from morning to sunset when I have watched its veiled
rising, because I am a widow, barbarous
and sun-cured in the face, I loved them ever since

I worked as a hand in Colonel Cody's circus,
under a great canvas larger than all their tents,
when they were paid to ride round in howling circles,

with a dime for their glory, and boys screamed in fright
at the galloping braves. Now the aspens enclose
the lances of rain, and the wet leaves shake with light."

From the fort another waltz drifted on the lake
past the pier's paper lanterns, swayed by violins
in the brass-buttoned night. Catherine Weldon,

like Achille on the river, watched the worried lines
made by the boathouse lanterns. Then she heard a loon's
wooden cry over black water. Lights draped the coigns

of the pierhead, then a scream as round as the moon's
circled her scalp. The nausea stirring her loins
was not from war, but from the treachery that came after

war, the white peace of paper so ornately signed
that perhaps that sound was really the loon's laughter
at treaties changing like clouds, their ink faded like wind.

Empires practised their abstract universals
of deceit: treaties signed with a wink of a pen's
eye dipped in an inkhorn, but this was not Versailles

with painted cherubs, but on the Dakota Plains.
She had believed in the redemptions of History,
that the papers the Sioux had folded to their hearts

would be kept like God's word, that each signatory,
after all that suffering, had blotted out their hates,
and that peace would break out as widely as the moon

through the black smoke of clouds that made the lake-water
shine stronger than the lanterns. Then she heard the loon,
no pain in the cry this time, but wooden laughter.

The clouds turned blank pages, the book I was reading
was like Plunkett charting the Battle of the Saints.
The New World was wide enough for a new Eden

of various Adams. A smell of innocence
like that of the first heavy snow came off the page
as I inhaled the spine. She walked past the lanterns

where some bark canoes were moored to the landing stage,
then paused to look at the waltzers in their ghost dance,
then stood at the window clapping transparent hands.

When one grief afflicts us we choose a sharper grief
in hope that enormity will ease affliction,
so Catherine Weldon rose in high relief

through the thin page of a cloud, making a fiction
of my own loss. I was searching for characters,
and in her shawled voice I heard the snow that would be blown

when the wind covered the tracks of the Dakotas,
the Sioux, and the Crows; my sorrow had been replaced.
Like a swift over water, her pen's shadow raced.

"I have found, in bleached grass, the miniature horror
of a crow's skull. When dry corn rattles its bonnet,
does it mean the Blackfoot is preparing for war?

When the Crow sets his visage on Death, and round it
circles his eyes with moons, each one is a mirror
foretold by his palm. So, the bird's skull in the grass

transfixed me, parting the spears of dry corn, just as
it would your blond soldiers. As for the herds that graze
through lance-high grasses, drifting with the Dakotas,

are not the Sioux as uncertain of paradise,
when the grass darkens, as your corn-headed soldiers?
Doubt isn't the privilege of one complexion.

I look to the white church spire and often think,
Is the cross for them also? The resurrection
of their bodies? The snow and the blood that we drink

for our broken Word? Ask your wheat-headed soldiers.
The charm that rattles in the fists of the shamans
is a god, not a writhing snake, with its severed tail.

They believe a Great Wind will whirl them in its hands
by grasses that never die, springs that never fail,
that restore their souls like the clear-running Hebron."

Lantern light shines through the skin of an army tent
where her shadow asked its question. Catherine Weldon,
in our final letter to the Indian agent.

Chapter XXXVI

I

Museums endure; but *sic transit gloria*
agitates the leaf-light on their concrete benches
in the sculpture garden, where frock-tailed sparrows are

tagging notes to a pediment while finches
debate on a classic façade. Art has surrendered
to History with its whiff of formaldehyde.

Over a glass-case a scholarly beard renders
a clouding judgement. The freckle-faced sun outside
mugs through a window, and so I retrieve my breath

from a varnished portrait, take back my irises
from glaring insomniac Caesar, for whom death
by marble resolved the conspirator's crisis,

past immortal statues inviting me to die.
Out in fresh air, close to a Bayeux of ivy,
I smoked on the steps and read the calligraphy

of swallows. Behind me, reverential mourners
whispered like people in banks or terminal wards;
Art is immortal and weighs heavily on us,

and museums leave us at a loss for words.
Outside becomes a museum: its ornate frames
square off a dome, a few trees, a brace of sparrows;

till every view is a postcard signed by great names:
that sky Canaletto's, that empty bench Van Gogh's.
I ground out my butt and re-entered the dead air,

down the echoing marble with its waxed air
of a pharaonic feast. Then round a corridor
I caught the light on green water as salt and clear

as the island's. Then I saw him. Achille! Bigger
than I remembered on the white sun-splintered deck
of the hot hull. Achille! My main man, my nigger!

circled by chain-sawing sharks; the ropes in his neck
turned his head towards Africa in *The Gulf Stream*,
which luffed him there, forever, between our island

and the coast of Guinea, fixed in the tribal dream,
in the light that entered another Homer's hand,
its breeze lifting the canvas from the museum.

But those leprous columns thudding against the hull
where Achille rests on one elbow always circle
his craft and mine, it needs no redemptive white sail

from a sea whose rhythm swells like Herman Melville.
Heah's Cap'n Melville on de whiteness ob de whale—
"Having for the imperial colour the same imperial hue . . .

giving the white man ideal mastership over every dusky tribe."
Lawd, Lawd, Massa Melville, what could a nigger do
but go down dem steps in de dusk you done describe?

So I stood in the dusk between the Greek columns
of the museum touched by the declining sun
on the gilt of the State House dome, on Saint Gaudens's

frieze of black soldiers darkening on the Common,
and felt myself melting in their dusk. My collar
turned up in a real freeze, I looked for a cab,

but cabs, like the fall, were a matter of colour,
and several passed, empty. In the back of one, Ahab
sat, trying to catch his whaler. I looped a shout

like a harpoon, like Queequeg, but the only spout
was a sculptured fountain's. *Sic transit* taxi, sport.
Streetlights came on. The museum windows went out.

Passing the lamplit leaves I knew I was different
from them as our skins were different in an empire
that boasted about its hues, in a New England

that had raked the leaves of the tribes into one fire
on the lawn back of the carport, like dead almond
leaves on a beach, and I saw the alarmed pale look,

when I stepped out of a streetlight, that a woman
gave me at a bus-stop, straight out of Melville's book;
then the consoling smile, like a shark's, all the fear

that had widened between us was incurable,
as cold as the edge of autumn in the night air
whose leaves rustled the pages of Melville's Bible.

I I I

White sanderlings scuttered towards the fraying net
of the evening surf, then panicked, just out of reach,
when a wave made another try, although it could not

exceed the limits set by the scalloping beach
where the birds were mirrored in slate, their shapes exact
and nervous, beaks darting, and then the wrinkling glass

disturbed their reflection. As I steadily walked
towards them, the clattering flock, to let me pass,
circled the tilted sea, and then it resettled,

wave, sand, and bird repeating their process, since they
had seen so many lovers joined by the hands, led
by the star that rises first from the darkening bay.

On the mud-marked seafront people took evening walks,
letting their dogs sniff the foam from a pewter surf,
gulls puffed their chests to the medalling sun on rocks

drying at low tide. Loosened kale heaved in the sough
of the lobster-yawls. A dog kept barking, "Hough, hough!"
at the stiff horizon. Homer (first name Winslow)

made that white chapel stroke under the mackerel-shoaled
sky of Marblehead, reframed in the windscreens
of cars in the parking lot. Summer was bone-cold.

On the nibbling beach whipped by its wind-machines
the scarves lifted and rattled with a lifeguard's flag,
and a knife that was edged with autumn pressed its blade

on my cheek, the wind sounded like a paper-bag
thwacked open, and the crunching sound my shoes made
on the concrete's sand enraged me. Tears blurred my sight;

head lowered, I stopped. White shoes were blocking my path.
I looked up. My father stood in the white drill suit
of his eternal summer on another wharf.

He stood in cold mud watching the curled froth decline
round Marblehead. Gulls were turning in from the cold.
He put out his hand. The palm was as cold as mine.

I said: "This is hardly the place; maybe I called
but it's too cold for talk; this happens to old men,
and I'm nearly there. You could have been my child,

186

and the more I live, the more our ages widen."
"We could go to a warmer place." My father smiled.
"Oh, not where you think, an island close to Eden.

But before you return, you must enter cities
that open like *The World's Classics*, in which I dreamt
I saw my shadow on their flagstones, histories

that carried me over the bridge of self-contempt,
though I never stared in their rivers, great abbeys
soaring in net-webbed stone, when I felt diminished

even by a postcard. Those things I wrote to please
your mother and our friends, unrevised, unfinished,
in drawing-room concerts died in their own applause.

Way back in the days of the barber's winding sheet,
I longed for those streets that History had made great,
but the island became my fortress and retreat,

in that circle of friends that I could dominate.
Dominate, Dominus. With His privilege,
I felt like the "I" that looks down on an island,

the way that a crested palm looks down from its ridge
on a harbour warmer than this one, or my hand.
But there is pride in cities, so remember this:

Once you have seen everything and gone everywhere,
cherish our island for its green simplicities,
enthrone yourself, if your sheet is a barber-chair,

a sail leaving harbour and a sail coming in,
the shadows of grape-leaves on sunlit verandahs
made me content. The sea-swift vanishes in rain,

and yet in its travelling all that the sea-swift does
it does in a circular pattern. Remember that, son."
The surf was dark. The lights stuttered in the windows

along the empty beach, red and green lights tossed on
the cold harbour, and beyond them, like dominoes
with lights for holes, the black skyscrapers of Boston.

BOOK FIVE

Chapter XXXVII

I

I crossed my meridian. Rust terraces, olive trees,
the grey horns of a port. Then, from a cobbled corner
of this mud-caked settlement founded by Ulysses—

swifts, launched from the nesting sills of Ulissibona,
their cries modulated to "Lisbon" as the Mediterranean
aged into the white Atlantic, their flight, in reverse,

repeating the X of an hourglass, every twitter an aeon
from which a horizon climbed in the upturned vase.
A church clock spun back its helm. Turtleback alleys

crawled from the sea, not towards it, to resettle
in the courtyard under the olives, and a breeze
turned over the leaves to show their silvery metal.

Here, clouds read backwards, muffling the clash
of church bells in cotton. There, on an opposite wharf,
Sunday in a cream suit, with a grey horned moustache,

strolled past wooden crates, and the long-shadowed Sabbath
was no longer Lisbon but Port of Spain. There, time sifts
like grain from a jute sack under the crooning pigeons.

Sunday clicks open a gold watch, startling the swifts
from the opening eye of a tower, closes it, then slips the sun's
pendulum back into its fob, patting it with a nod.

Sunday strolls past a warehouse whose iron-ringed door
exhales an odor of coffee as a reek of salt cod
slithers through the railings. Sunday is a widower

in an ice-cream suit, and a straw with a mourning band,
an old Portugee leathery as Portugal, via Madeira,
with a stalled watch for a compass. When he rewinds its hand

it raises an uproar of docks, mulatto clerks cowed
by jets of abuse from wine-barrelled wholesalers,
winches and cranes, black drivers cursing black loaders,

and gold-manacled vendors teasing the Vincentian sailors
folded over the hulls. Then not a single word, as
Saturday went home at one, except from the pigeons

and a boy rattling his stick along the rusted staves
of a railing, its bars caging him as he runs.
After that arpeggio, Sunday hears his own footsteps,

making centuries recede, the ebbing market in slaves
and sugar declining below the horizon. Then Sunday stops
to hear schooners thudding on overlapping wharves.

Across the meridian, I try seeing the other side,
past rusty containers, waves like welts from the lash
in a light as clear as oil from the olive seed.

Once the world's green gourd was split like a calabash
by Pope Alexander's decree. Spices, vanilla
sweetened this wharf; the grain of swifts would scatter

in their unchanging pattern, their cries no shriller
than they are now over the past, or ours, for that matter,
if our roles were reversed, and the sand in one half

replicated the sand in the other. Now I had come
to a place I felt I had known, an antipodal wharf
where my forked shadow swayed to the same brass pendulum.

Yes, but not as one of those pilgrims whose veneration carried
the salt of their eyes up the grooves of a column
to the blue where forked swifts navigated. Far from it; instead,

I saw how my shadow detached itself from them
when it disembarked on the wharf through a golden haze
of corn from another coast. My throat was scarred

from a horizon that linked me to others, when our eyes
lowered to the cobbles that climbed to the castle yard,
when the coins of the olives showed us their sovereign's face.

My shadow had preceded me. How else could it recognize
that light to which it was attached, this port where Europe
rose with its terrors and terraces, slope after slope?

A bronze horseman halts at a wharf, his green-bronze
cloak flecked with white droppings, his wedged visor
shading the sockets' hyphenating horizons,

his stare fixed like a helm. We had no such erections
above our colonial wharves, our erogenous zones
were not drawn to power, our squares shrank the directions

of the Empire's plazas. Above us, no stallions paw
the sky's pavement to strike stars from the stones,
no sword is pointed to recapture the port of Genoa.

There the past is an infinite Sunday. It's hot, or it rains;
the sun lifts the sheets of the rain, and the gutters
run out. For those to whom history is the presence

of ruins, there is a green nothing. No bell tower utters
its flotilla of swallows memorizing an alphabet,
no cobbles crawl towards the sea. We think of the past

as better forgotten than fixed with stony regret.
Here, a castle in the olives rises over the tiered roofs
of crusted tile but, like the stone Don in the opera,

is the ghost of itself. Over the flagstones, hooves
clop down from the courtyard, stuttering pennons appear
from the mouths of arches, and the past dryly grieves

from the O's of a Roman aqueduct; silver cuirasses
flash in the reversible olives, their silvery leaves,
and twilight ripens the municipal canvases,

where, one knee folded, like a drinking deer, an admiral
with a grey horned moustache and foam collar proffers a gift
of plumed Indians and slaves. The wharves of Portugal

were empty as those of the islands. The slate pigeons lift
from the roof of a Levantine warehouse, the castle in the trees
is its own headstone. Yet, once, Alexander's meridian

gave half a gourd to Lisbon, the seeds of its races,
and half to Imperial Spain. Now Sunday afternoon passes
the empty cafés, their beads hanging like rosaries,

as shawled fado singers sob in turn to their mandolins
while a cobbled lane climbs like a tortoise, and tiredly raises
its head of a pope at the limp sails on washing lines.

Chapter XXXVIII

I

In scorched summer light, from the circle of Charing Cross,
he arose with the Underground's grit and its embers of sparrows
in a bargeman's black greatcoat, clutching in one scrofulous

claw his brown paper manuscript. The nose, like a pharos,
bulbed from his cragged face, and the beard under it was
foam that exploded into the spray burst of eyebrows.

On the verge of collapse, the fallen sails of his trousers
were upheld by a rope. In the barges of different shoes
he flapped towards the National. The winch of his voice,

a fog still in its throat, barged through the queues
at the newspaper kiosks, then changed gears with the noise
of red double-deckers embarking on chartered views

from pigeon-stirred Trafalgar; it broke off the icing
from wedding-cake London. Gryphons on their ridge
of sandstone snarled because it had carried the cries in

the Isle of Dogs running over Westminster Bridge.
Today it would anchor in the stone waves of the entrance
of St. Martin-in-the-Fields. There, in tiered sunshine,

the black sail collapsed, face sunward with both hands
crossed over the shop-paper volume bound with grey twine.
He looked like a heap of slag-coal crusting the tiers

with their summering tourists. Eyes shut, the frayed lips
chewed the breeze, the beard curled like the dog's ears
of his turned-down *Odyssey*, but Omeros was naming the ships

whose oars spidered soundlessly over the sun-webbed calm
behind his own lashes. Then, suddenly, a raging sparrow
of a church-warden bobbed down the steps. It picked one arm.

The bargeman huddled. It screeched. It yanked an elbow,
then kicked him with polished pumps, and a curse as
Greek to the choleric cleric as one might imagine

sprayed the spluttering soutane. It showed him the verses
framed at the entrance announcing this Sunday's lesson
in charity, etc. Then, like a dromedary, over the sands

of the scorching pavement, the hump began to press on
back to the river. The sparrow, rubbing both hands,
nodded, and chirruped up the steps back to its sanctuary,

where, dipping one claw in the font, it vanished inside
the webbed stone. The bargeman tacked towards his estuary
of light. It was summer. London rustled with pride.

II

He curled up on a bench underneath the Embankment wall.
He saw London gliding with the Thames around its neck
like a barge which an old brown horse draws up a canal

if its yoke is Time. From here he could see the dreck
under the scrolled skirts of statues, the grit in the stone lions'
eyes; he saw under everything an underlying grime

that itched in the balls of rearing bronze stallions,
how the stare of somnolent sphinxes closed in time
to the swaying bells of "cities all the floure"

petalling the spear-railed park where a couple suns
near the angled shade of All-Hallows by the Tower,
as the tinkling Thames drags by in its ankle-irons,

while the ginkgo's leaves flexed their fingers overhead.
He mutters its fluent alphabet, the peaked A of a spire,
the half-vowels of bridges, down to the crumpled Z

of his overcoat draping a bench in midsummer's fire.
He read the inverted names of boats in their element,
he saw the tugs chirring up a devalued empire

as the coins of their wake passed the Houses of Parliament.
But the shadows keep multiplying from the Outer
Provinces, their dialects light as the ginkgo's leaf, their

195

fingers plucking their saris as wind picks at water,
and the statues raising objections; he sees a wide river
with its landing of pier-stakes flooding Westminster's

flagstones, and traces the wake of dugouts in the frieze
of a bank's running cornice, and whenever the ginkgo stirs
the wash of far navies settles in the bargeman's eyes.

A statue swims upside down, one hand up in response
to a question raised in the House, and applause rises
from the clapping Thames, from benches in the leaves.

And the sunflower sets after all, retracting its irises
with the bargeman's own, then buds on black, iron trees
as a gliding fog hides the empires: London, Rome, Greece.

III

Who decrees a great epoch? The meridian of Greenwich.
Who doles out our zeal, and in which way lies our
hope? In the cobbles of sinister Shoreditch,

in the widening rings of Big Ben's iron flower,
in the barges chained like our islands to the Thames.
Where is the alchemical corn and the light it yields?

Where, in which stones of the Abbey, are incised our names?
Who defines our delight? St. Martin-in-the-Fields.
After every Michaelmas, its piercing soprano steeple

defines our delight. Within whose palatable vault
will echo the Saints' litany of our island people?
St. Paul's salt shaker, when we are worth their salt.

Stand by the tilted crosses of well-quiet Glen-da-Lough.
Follow the rook's crook'd finger to the ivied grange.
As black as the rook is, it comes from a higher stock.

Who screams out our price? The crows of the Corn Exchange.
Where are the pleasant pastures? A green baize-table.
Who invests in our happiness? The Chartered Tour.

Who will teach us a history of which we too are capable?
The red double-decker's view of the Bloody Tower.
When are our brood, like the sparrows, a public nuisance?

When they screech at the sinuous swans on the Serpentine.
The swans are royally protected, but in whose hands
are the black crusts of our children? In the pointing sign

under the harps of the willows, to the litter of Margate Sands.
What has all this to do with the price of fish, our salary
tidally scanned with the bank-rate by waxworks tellers?

Where is the light of the world? In the National Gallery.
In Palladian Wren. In the City that can buy and sell us
the packets of tea stirred with our crystals of sweat.

Where is our sublunar peace? In that sickle sovereign
peeling the gilt from St. Paul's onion silhouette.
There is our lunar peace: in the glittering grain

of the coined estuary, our moonlit, immortal wheat,
its white sail cresting the gradual swell of the Downs,
startling the hare from the pillars on Salisbury Plain,

sharpening the grimaces of thin-lipped market towns,
whitewashing the walls of Brixton, darkening the grain
when coal-shadows cross it. Dark future down darker street.

Chapter XXXIX

I

The great headstones lifted like the keels of curraghs
from Ireland's groundswell and spray foamed on the walls
of the broken abbey. That silver was the lake's,

a salver held by a tonsured hill. The old well's
silence increased as gravel was crunched by pilgrims
following the monks' footpath. Silence was in flower.

It widened the furrows like a gap between hymns,
if that pause were protracted hour after hour
by century-ringed oaks, by a square Celtic cross,

by wafers of snowdrops from the day webbed mortar
had cinched the stone to the whisk of a sorrel horse
grazing its station. In it, a paper aspen

rustled its missal. Its encircling power
lifted the midges in vertiginous Latin,
then sailed a rook into the slit of a tower

like a card in a post-box. It waxed a tea-van,
draped a booth with sweaters, then it crossed the dry road
to hear a brook talk the old language of Ireland.

There it filled a bucket and carried the clear load
for the sorrel to nuzzle with ruffling nostrils.
The weight of the place, its handle, its ancient name

for "wood with a lake," or "abbey with hooded hills,"
rooted in the bucket's clang, echoed the old shame
of disenfranchisement. I had no oasis,

no pebbled language to drink from like a calm horse
or pilgrim lapping up soul-watering places;
the grass was brighter with envy, then my remorse

was a clouding sun. The sorrel swaying its whisk,
the panes of blue sky in the abbey were all set
in a past as old as Glen-da-Lough's obelisk,

when alder and aspen aged in one alphabet.
The child-voiced brook repeated History's lesson
as an elder clapped its leaves in approbation

until others swayed to the old self-possession
for which faith is known; but which faith, in a nation
split by a glottal scream, by a sparrow's chirrup,

where a prayer incised in a cross, a Celtic rune
could send the horse circling with empty stirrup
from a sniper's bolt? Here, from this abbey's ruin,

if the rook flew north with its funereal caw,
far from this baptismal font, this silver weir,
too high for inspection as it crossed the border,

it would see a street that ended in wreaths of wire
while a hearse with drizzling lights waits for an order
in a sharp accent, making the black boots move on

in scraping syllables, the gun on its shoulder,
still splitting heirs, dividing a Shem from a Shaun,
an Ireland no wiser as it got older.

Though all its wiry hedgerows startle the spirit,
when the ancient letters rise to a tinker's spoon,
banging a saucepan, those fields which they inherit

hide stones white-knuckled with hatred. A pitted moon
mounted the green pulpit of Sugar Loaf Mountain
in its wax-collar. Along a yew-guarded road,

a cloud hung from a branch in the orange hour,
like a shirt that was stained with poetry and with blood.
The wick of the cypress charred. Glen-da-Lough's tower.

III

I leant on the mossed embankment just as if he
bloomed there every dusk with eye-patch and tilted hat,
rakish cane on one shoulder. Along the Liffey,

the mansards dimmed to one indigo silhouette;
then a stroke of light brushed the honey-haired river,
and there, in black cloche hat and coat, she scurried faster

to the changing rose of a light. Anna Livia!
Muse of our age's Omeros, undimmed Master
and true tenor of the place! So where was my gaunt,

cane-twirling flaneur? I blest myself in his voice,
and climbed up the wooden stairs to the restaurant
with its brass spigots, its glints, its beer-brightened noise.

"There's a bower of roses by Bendemeer's stream"
was one of the airs Maud Plunkett played, from Moore
perhaps, and I murmured along with them; its theme,

as each felted oar lifted and dipped with hammer-
like strokes, was that of an adoring sunflower
turning bright hair to her Major. And then I saw him.

The Dead were singing in fringed shawls, the wick-low shade
leapt high and rouged their cold cheeks with vermilion
round the pub piano, the air Maud Plunkett played,

rowing her with felt hammer-strokes from my island
to one with bright doors and cobbles, and then Mr. Joyce
led us all, as gently as Howth when it drizzles,

his voice like sun-drizzled Howth, its violet lees
of moss at low tide, where a dog barks "Howth! Howth!" at
the shawled waves, and the stone I rubbed in my pocket

from the Martello brought one-eyed Ulysses
to the copper-bright strand, watching the mail-packet
butting past the Head, its wake glittering like keys.

Chapter XL

I

A snail gnawing a leaf, the mail-packet nibbles
the Aegean coast, its wake a caterpillar's
accordion. Then, becalmed by its own ripples,

sticks like a butterfly to its branch. The pillars,
the lizard-crossed terraces on the ruined hills
are as quiet as the sail. Storks crest the columns.

Gulls chalk the blue enamel and a hornet drills
the pink blossoms of the oleander and hums
at its work. In white villages with cracked plaster

walls, shawled women lean quietly on their shadows,
remembering statues in their alabaster
manhood, when their oiled hair was parted like the crow's

folded wings. The flutes in the square and the sea-lace
of bridal lilac; sawing fiddles that outlast
the cicadas. On the scorched deck Odysseus

hears the hill music through the wormholes of the mast.
The sail clings like a butterfly to the elbow
of an olive branch. A bride on her father's arm

scared of her future. On its tired shadow,
the prow turns slowly, uncertain of its aim.
He peels his sunburnt skin in maps of grey parchment

which he scrolls absently between finger and thumb.
The crew stare like statues at that feigned detachment
whose heart, in its ribs, thuds like the galley-slaves' drum.

II

Hunched on their oars, they smile; "This is we Calypso,
Captain, who treat we like swine, you ain't seeing shore.
Let this sun burn you black and blister your lips so

it hurt them to give orders, fuck you and your war."
The mattock rests, idle. No oar lifts a finger.
Blisters flower on palms. The bewildered trireme

is turning the wrong way, like the cloud-eyed singer
whose hand plucked the sea's wires, back towards the dream
of Helen, back to that island where their hunched spine

bristled and they foraged the middens of Circe,
when her long white arm poured out the enchanting wine
and they bucked in cool sheets. "Cap'n, boy? Beg mercy

o' that breeze for a change, because sometimes your heart
is as hard as that mast, you dream of Ithaca,
you pray to your gods. May they be as far apart

from your wandering as ours in Africa.
Island after island passing. Still we ain't home."
The boatswain lifted the mattock, and the metre

of the long oars slowly settled on a rhythm
as the prow righted. He saw a limestone palace
over his small harbour, he saw a sea-swift skim

the sun-harped water, and felt the ant of a breeze
crossing his forehead, and now the caterpillar's
strokes of the oars lifted the fanning chrysalis

of the full sails as a wake was sheared by the bow.
The quick mattock beat like the heart of Odysseus;
and if you have seen a butterfly steer its shadow

across a hot cove at noon or a rigged canoe
head for the horns of an island, then you will know
why a harbour-mouth opens with joy, why black crew,

slaves, and captain at the end of their enterprise
shouted in response as they felt the troughs lifting
and falling with their hearts, why rowers closed their eyes

and prayed they were headed home. They knew the drifting
Caribbean currents from Andros to Castries
might drag them to Margarita or Curaçao,

that the nearer home, the deeper our fears increase,
that no house might come to meet us on our own shore,
and fishermen fear this as much as Ulysses

until they see the single eye of the lighthouse
winking at them. Then the strokes match heartbeat to oar,
their blistered palms weeping for palms or olive trees.

III

And Istanbul's spires, each dome a burnoosed Turk,
swathed like a Saracen, with the curved scimitar
of a crescent moon over it, or the floating muck

of a lowering Venice probed by a gondolier,
rippling lines repeating some pilgrim's journals,
the weight of cities that I found so hard to bear;

in them was the terror of Time, that I would march
with columns at twilight, only to disappear
into a past whose history echoed the arch

of bridges sighing over their ancient canals
for a place that was not mine, since what I preferred
was not statues but the bird in the statue's hair.

The honeyed twilight cupped in long, shadowed squares,
the dripping dungeons, the idiot dukes, were all
redeemed by the creamy strokes of a Velázquez,

like the scraping cellos in concentration camps,
with art next door to the ovens, the fluting veil
of smoke soaring with Schubert? The cracked glass of Duchamp's

The Bride Stripped Bare by Her Bachelors; did Dada
foresee the future of Celan and Max Jacob
as part of the cosmic midden? What my father

spiritedly spoke of was that other Europe
of mausoleum museums, the barber's shelf
of *The World's Great Classics*, with a vanity whose

spires and bells punctually pardoned itself
in the absolution of fountains and statues,
in writhing, astonishing tritons; their cold noise

brimming the basin's rim, repeating that power
and art were the same, from some Caesar's eaten nose
to spires at sunset in the swift's half-hour.

Tell that to a slave from the outer regions
of their fraying empires, what power lay in the work
of forgiving fountains with naiads and lions.

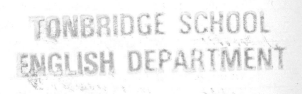

Chapter XLI

Service. Under my new empire. The Romans
acquired Greek slaves as aesthetics instructors
of their spoilt children, many from obscure islands

of their freshly acquired archipelago. But those tutors,
curly-haired, served a state without equestrians
apart from statues; a republic without class,

tiered only on wealth, and eaten with prejudice
from its pillared base, the Athenian *demos*,
its *demos* demonic and its *ocracy* crass,

corrupting the blue-veined marble with its disease,
stillborn as a corpse, for all those ideals went cold
in the heat of its hate. And not only in tense

Southern towns and plantations, where it often killed
the slaves it gave Roman names for dumb insolence,
small squares with Athenian principles and pillars

maintained by convicts and emigrants who had fled
persecution and gave themselves *fasces* with laws
to persecute slaves. A wedding-cake Republic.

Its domes, museums, its ornate institutions,
its pillared façade that looked down on the black
shadows that they cast as an enraging nuisance

which, if it were left to its Solons, with enough luck
would vanish from its cities, just as the Indians
had vanished from its hills. Leaves on an autumn rake.

I I

I re-entered my reversible world. Its opposite
lay in the autumnal lake whose trees kept still
perfectly, but where my disembodied trunk split

along the same line of reflection that halved Achille,
since men's shadows are not pieces moved by a frown,
by the same hand that opens the willow's fan to the light,

indifferent to who lifts us up once we are put down,
fixed in hierarchical postures, pawn, bishop, knight,
nor are we simply chameleons, self-dyeing our skins

to each background. The widening mind can acquire
the hues of a foliage different from where it begins
in the low hills of Gloucester running with smokeless fire.

There Iroquois flashed in the Indian red, in the sepias
and ochres of leaf-mulch, the mind dyed from the stain
on their sacred ground, the smoke-prayer of the tepees

pushed back by the Pilgrim's pitchfork. All over again,
diaspora, exodus, when the hills in their piebald ranges
move like their ponies, the tribes moving like trees

downhill to the lowland, a flag-fading smoke-wisp estranges
them. First men, then the forests. Until the earth
lies barren as the dusty Dakotas. Men take their colours

as the trees do from the native soil of their birth,
and once they are moved elsewhere, entire cultures
lose the art of mimicry, and then, where the trees were,

the fir, the palm, the olive, the cedar, a desert place
widens in the heart. This is the first wisdom of Caesar,
to change the ground under the bare soles of a race.

This was the groan of the autumn wind in the tamaracks
which I shared through Catherine's body, coming in waves
through the leaves of the Shawmut, the ochre hands of the Aruacs.

Here too, at Concord, the contagious vermilion
advanced with the maples, like red poinciana
under the fort of that lion-headed island,

spreading the stain on a map under the banner
of a cloud-wigged George. Under the planks of its bridge
the mossed logs lay with black shakos like dead Hussars.

The shot heard round the world entered the foliage
of Plunkett's redoubt, when the arc of an empire was
flung over both colonies, wider than the seine

a fisherman hurls over a bay at sunrise,
but all colonies inherit their empire's sin,
and these, who broke free of the net, enmeshed a race.

Cicadas exchanged musket-volleys in the wood.
A log held fire. To orders from an insane
cloud, battalions of leaves kept falling in their blood.

Flare fast and fall, Indian flags of October!
The blue or grey waves riding in Boston Harbor,
the tide like the cavalry, with its streaming mane

and its cirrus-pennons; ripen the grape-arbour
with its thick trellis; redden the sumac from Maine
to the Finger Lakes, let the hornet keep drilling

forts of firewood and mitred Hussars stand by
in scarlet platoons, signed on for George's shilling,
let aspens lift their aprons and flutter goodbye,

let the earth fold over from the Pilgrim's sober
plough, raise pitchforks to scatter your daughters out of
the hayloft, erect your white steeple over

the cowed pews, lift the Book, whose wrinkled cover
is Leviathan's hide; damn them and their love, or
hurl the roped lance in the heart of Jehovah!

That was Catherine's terror; the collar, the hay-rake,
the evening hymn in the whalehouse, its starched ribs
white as a skeleton. The nightmare cannot wake

from a Sunday where the mouse-claw of ivy grips
the grooved brick of colleges, while a yellow tractor
breaks the Sabbath and the alchemical plateau

of the Transcendental New England character,
sifting wit from the chaff, the thorn out of Thoreau,
the mess from Emerson, where a benefactor

now bronzed in his unshifting principles can show
us that any statue is a greater actor
than its original by its longer shadow.

Privileges did not separate me, instead
they linked me closer to them by that mental chain
whose eyes interlocked with mine, as if we all stood

at a lectern or auction block. Their condition
the same, without manacles. The chains were subtler,
but they were still hammered out of the white-hot forge

that made every captor a blacksmith. The river
had been crossed, but the chain-links of eyes in each face
still flashed submission or rage; I saw distance

in them, and it wearied me; I saw what Achille
had seen and heard: the metal eyes joining their hands
to wrists adept with an oar or a "special skill."

Chapter XLII

I

Acres of synonymous lights, black battery cells
and terminals coiling with traffic, winked out. Sunrise
reddened the steel lake. Downstairs, in the hotel's

Canadian-fall window, a young Polish waitress with eyes
wet as new coal and a pageboy haircut was pouring him
coffee, the maples in glass as yellow as orange juice.

Her porcelain wrist tilted, filling his gaze to the brim.
He hoped adoration unnerved her; the sensible shoes
skirting the bare tables, her hand aligning the service

with finical clicks. As if it had tapped her twice
on the back for her papers, she turned with that nervous
smile of the recent immigrant that borders on tears.

A Polish Sunday enclosed it. A Baroque square, its age
patrolled by young soldiers, the flag of their sagging regime
once bright as her lipstick, the consonants of a language

crunched by their boot soles. In it was the scream
of a kettle leaving a freightyard, then the soft farms
with horses and willows nodding past a train window,

the queues in the drizzle. Then the forms
where her name ran over the margin, then a passport photo
where her scared face waited when she opened its door.

She was part of that pitiless fiction so common now
that it carried her wintry beauty into Canada,
it lined her eyelashes with the snow's blue shadow,

it made her slant cheekbones flash like the cutlery
in the hope of a newer life. At the cashier's machine
she stood like a birch at the altar, and, very quietly,

snow draped its bridal lace over the raven's-wing sheen.
Her name melted in mine like flakes on a river
or a black pond in which the wind shakes packets of milk.

When she stood with the cheque, I tried reading the glow
of brass letters on her blouse. Her skin, shaded in silk,
smelt fresh as a country winter before the first snow.

Snow brightened the linen, the pepper, salt domes, the gables
of the napkin, silencing Warsaw, feathering quiet Cracow;
then the raven's wing flew again between the white tables.

There are days when, however simple the future, we do not go
towards it but leave part of life in a lobby whose elevators
divide and enclose us, brightening digits that show

exactly where we are headed, while a young Polish waitress
is emptying an ashtray, and we are drawn to a window
whose strings, if we pull them, widen an emptiness.

We yank the iron-grey drapes, and the screeching pulleys
reveal in the silence not fall in Toronto
but a city whose language was seized by its police,

that other servitude Nina Something was born into,
where under gun-barrel chimneys the smoke holds its voice
till it rises with hers. Zagajewski. Herbert. Milosz.

I I

November. Sober month. The leaves' fling was over.
Willows harped on the Charles, their branches would blacken.
Drizzles gusted on bridges, lights came on earlier,

twigs clawed the clouds, the hedges turned into bracken,
the sky raced like a shaggy wolf with a rabbit pinned
in its jaws, its fur flying with the first snow,

then gnawed at the twilight with its incisors skinned;
the light bled, flour flew past the grey window.
I saw Catherine Weldon running in the shawled wind.

The ghost dance of winter was about to start.
The snowflakes pressed their patterns on the crusting panes,
lakes hardened with ice, a lantern lit the wolf's heart,

the grass hibernated under obdurate pines,
light sank in the earth as the growing thunderhead
in its army blanket travelled the Great Plains,

with lightning lance, flour-faced, crow-bonneted,
but carrying its own death inside it, wearily.
Red god gone with autumn and white winter early.

Chapter XLIII

I

Flour was falling on the Plains. Her hair turned grey
carrying logs from the woodpile. The tiny turret
of the fort in the snow pointed like a chalet

in a child's crystal and Catherine remembered
the lights on all afternoon in a Boston street,
the power of the globe that lay in a girl's palm

to shake the world to whiteness and obliterate
it the way the drifts were blurring the Parkin farm,
the orange twilight cast by the feverish grate

at the carpet's edge on arrows of andirons
in a brass quiver. She felt the light marking lines
on her warm forehead, reddening the snow mountains

above the chalet with their green crepe-paper pines;
then she would shake the crystal and all would be snow,
the Ghost Dance, assembling then, as it was now.

Work made her wrists cold iron. She rested the axe
down in its white echo. No life was as hard as
the Sioux's, she thought. But a pride had stiffened their backs.

Hunger could shovel them up like dried cicadas
into the fiery pit like that in the hearth,
when she stared round-eyed in the flames. They were not meek,

and she had been taught the meek inherit the earth.
The flour kept falling. Inedible manna
fell on their children's tongues, from dribbling sacks

condemned by the army. The crow's flapping banner
flew over the homes of the Braves. They stood like stakes
without wires: the Crows, the Sioux, the Dakotas.

The snow blew in their wincing faces like papers
from another treaty which a blind shaman tears
to bits in the wind. The pines have lifted their spears.

Except that the thick, serrated line on the slope
was rapidly growing more pine-trees. A faint bugle
sounded from the chalet. She watched the pine-trees slip

in their white smoke downhill to the hoot of an owl
and yapping coyotes answering the bugle,
as the pines lowered their lances in a gallop,

and she heard what leapt from the pine-logs as a girl,
the crackle of rifle-fire from the toy fort,
like cicadas in drought; then she heard the cannon—

the late muffled echo after it was fired
and the dark blossom it made, its arch bringing down
lances and riders with it. The serrated sea

of pines spread out on the plain, their own avalanche
whitening them, but they screamed in the ecstasy
of their own massacre, since this was the Ghost Dance,

and the blizzard slowly erased their swirling cries,
the horses and spinning riders with useless shields,
in the white smoke, the Sioux, the Dakotas, the Crows.

The flour basting their corpses on the white fields.
The absence that settled over the Dakotas
was contained in the globe. Its pines, its tiny house.

I I

"I pray to God that I never share in man's will,
which widened before me. I saw a chain of men
linked by wrists to our cavalry. I watched until

they were a line of red ants. I let out a moan
as the last ant disappeared. Then I rode downhill
away from the Parkin farm to the Indian camp.

I entered the camp in the snow. A starved mongrel
and a papoose sat in the white street, with a clay
vessel in the child's hands, and the dog's fanged growl

backed off from my horse, then lunged. Then I turned away
down another street through the tents to more and more
silence. There were hoof-marks frozen in the flour dust

near a hungry tent-mouth. I got off. Through its door
I saw white-eyed Omeros, motionless. He must
be deaf too, I thought, as well as blind, since his head

never turned, and then he lifted the dry rattle
in one hand, and it was the same sound I had heard
in Cody's circus, the snake hiss before battle.

There was a broken arrow, and others in the quiver
around his knees. Those were our promises. I stared
a long while at his silence. It was a white river

under black pines in winter. I was only scared
when my horse snorted outside, perhaps from the sound
of the rattler. I went back outside. Where were the

women and children? I walked on the piebald ground
with its filthy snow, and stopped. I saw a warrior
frozen in a drift and took him to be a Sioux

and heard the torn war flags rattling on their poles,
then the child's cry somewhere in the flour of snow,
but never found her or the dog. I saw the soles

of their moccasins around the tents, and a horse
ribbed like a barrel with flies circling its teeth.
I walked like a Helen among their dead warriors.

"This was history. I had no power to change it.
And yet I still felt that this had happened before.
I knew it would happen again, but how strange it

was to have seen it in Boston, in the hearth-fire.
I was a leaf in the whirlwind of the Ordained.
Then Omeros's voice came from the mouth of the tent:

'We galloped towards death swept by the exaltation
of meeting ourselves in a place just like this one:
The Ghost Dance has tied the tribes into one nation.

As the salmon grows tired of its ladder of stone,
so have we of fighting the claws of the White Bear,
dripping red beads on the snow. Whiteness is everywhere.' "

Look, Catherine! There are no more demons outside the door.
The white wolf drags its shawled tail into the high snow
through the pine lances, the blood dried round its jaw;

it is satisfied. Come, come to the crusted window,
blind as it is with the ice, through the pane's cataract;
see, it's finished. It's over, Catherine, you have been saved.

But she sat on a chair in the parlour while the cracked
window spread its webs, and for days and nights starved
and thinned in her rocker. The maddened wind runs

around the still farm. Bread greened, and like a carved
totem her body hardened to wood. Apples dried, onions
curled with green sprouts, and rats, growing bolder,

with eyes like berries, moved like the burial lanterns
of the cavalry. Her shawl slipped from one shoulder
but she left it there, in peace, since this was peace now,

the winter of the Ghost Dance. "I'm one year older,"
she said to the feathery window. "I loved snow
once, but now I dread its white siege outside my door."

Years severed in half by winter! By a darkness
through which branches groped, paralyzed in their distress.
Which flocks betrayed. Wild geese with their own honking noise

over jammed highways, the Charles's slow-moving ice.
No twilight, but lamps turned on in mid-afternoon,
my humped shadow like a bear entering its cave,

clawing at the frozen lock, as every noun
became its muffled echo, every street a grave
with snow on both sides. I caught the implications

of a traffic-light winking on an iron sky
that I could, since the only civilizations
were those with snow, whiten to anonymity.

Turn the page. Blank winter. The obliteration
of nouns fading into echoes, the alphabet
of scribbling branches. Boots stamp the trolley station.

Dead cars foam at the mouth with icicles. The boat
of the streetcar's light divides the frozen breakers,
then steaming passengers scratch at the webbed windows'

quickly stitched lace. Swaying in black coats and parkas,
every face is a lantern wincing when the doors
part their rubber accordion, their tears like glass.

The name I had mispronounced was as muffled now
as any white noun outside the spectral stations
along the line, where the faces were flecked with snow

when the full car passed them, resigned in their patience
like statues in their museum. Her old address
enlarged with the next stop. The passengers staggered

on the straps, the doors in a blast of malice
grinned open, the bell rang, and suddenly I stood
in bewildering whiteness, flakes clouding my eyes.

The streets were white as her studio, huge boulders
of sculptured coral, the blinding limestone of Greece
like frozen breakers on the path between closed doors.

The panes of ice in the gutters were as grey as
those of the houses. I climbed steps, I read buzzers,
searched from the pavement again for that attic where

a curved statue had rolled black stockings down its knees,
unclipped and then shaken the black rain of its hair,
and "Omeros" echoed from a white-throated vase.

But no door opened to show me her startled eyes
behind its brass chain, no light linked the Asian bones
of the axe-blade cheek. The glaucous windows were blind.

I had lost the address. I walked through coral stones
that whined like a cemetery in the sunlit wind,
then waited for the trolley's eye as we did once

on the other side of that year. One came. Its doors
yawned and rattled shut. Its hull slid past the combers.
Houses passed like a wharf. Hers. Or some other house.

BOOK SIX

Chapter XLIV

I

In hill-towns, from San Fernando to Mayagüez,
the same sunrise stirred the feathered lances of cane
down the archipelago's highways. The first breeze

rattled the spears and their noise was like distant rain
marching down from the hills, like a shell at your ears.
In the cool asphalt Sundays of the Antilles

the light brought the bitter history of sugar
across the squared fields, heightening towards harvest,
to the bleached flags of the Indian diaspora.

The drizzling light blew across the savannah
darkening the racehorses' hides; mist slowly erased
the royal palms on the crests of the hills and the

hills themselves. The brown patches the horses had grazed
shone as wet as their hides. A skittish stallion
jerked at his bridle, marble-eyed at the thunder

muffling the hills, but the groom was drawing him in
like a fisherman, wrapping the slack line under
one fist, then with the other tightening the rein

and narrowing the circle. The sky cracked asunder
and a forked tree flashed, and suddenly that black rain
which can lose an entire archipelago

in broad daylight was pouring tin nails on the roof,
hammering the balcony. I closed the French window,
and thought of the horses in their stalls with one hoof

tilted, watching the ropes of rain. I lay in bed
with current gone from the bed-lamp and heard the roar
of wind shaking the windows, and I remembered

Achille on his own mattress and desperate Hector
trying to save his canoe, I thought of Helen
as my island lost in the haze, and I was sure

I'd never see her again. All of a sudden
the rain stopped and I heard the sluicing of water
down the guttering. I opened the window when

the sun came out. It replaced the tiny brooms
of palms on the ridges. On the red galvanized
roof of the paddock, the wet sparkled, then the grooms

led the horses over the new grass and exercised
them again, and there was a different brightness
in everything, in the leaves, in the horses' eyes.

I smelt the leaves threshing at the top of the year
in green January over the orange villas
and military barracks where the Plunketts were,

the harbour flecked by the wind that comes with Christmas,
edged with the Arctic, that was christened *Vent Noël*;
it stayed until March and, with luck, until Easter.

It freshened the cedars, waxed the *laurier-cannelle*,
and hid the African swift. I smelt the drizzle
on the asphalt leaving the Morne, it was the smell

of an iron on damp cloth; I heard the sizzle
of fried jackfish in oil with their coppery skin;
I smelt ham studded with cloves, the crusted accra,

the wax in the varnished parlour: Come in. Come in,
the arm of the Morris chair sticky with lacquer;
I saw a sail going out and a sail coming in,

and a breeze so fresh it lifted the lace curtains
like a petticoat, like a sail towards Ithaca;
I smelt a dead rivulet in the clogged drains.

I I I

Ah, twin-headed January, seeing either tense:
a past, they assured us, born in degradation,
and a present that lifted us up with the wind's

noise in the breadfruit leaves with such an elation
that it contradicts what is past! The cannonballs
of rotting breadfruit from the Battle of the Saints,

the asterisks of bulletholes in the brick walls
of the redoubt. I lived there with every sense.
I smelt with my eyes, I could see with my nostrils.

Chapter XLV

I

One side of the coast plunges its precipices
into the Atlantic. Turns require wide locks,
since the shoulder is sharp and the curve just misses

a long drop over the wind-bent trees and the rocks
between the trees. There is a wide view of Dennery,
with its stone church and raw ochre cliffs at whose base

the African breakers end. Across the flecked sea
whose combers veil and unveil the rocks with their lace
the next port is Dakar. The uninterrupted wind

thuds under the wings of frigates, you see them bent
from a force that has crossed the world, tilting to find
purchase in the sudden downdrafts of its current.

The breeze threshed the palms on the cool December road
where the Comet hurtled with empty leopard seats,
so fast a man on a donkey trying to read

its oncoming fiery sign heard only two thudding beats
from the up-tempo *zouk* that its stereo played
when it screeched round a bridge and began to ascend

away from the palm-fronds and their wickerwork shade
that left the windscreen clear as it locked round the bend,
where Hector suddenly saw the trotting piglet

and thought of Plunkett's warning as he heard it screel
with the same sound that the tires of the Comet
made rounding the curve from the sweat-greased steering wheel.

The rear wheels spin to a dead stop, like a helm.
The piglet trots down the safer side of the road.
Lodged in their broken branches the curled letters flame.

Hector had both hands on the wheel. His head was bowed
under the swaying statue of the Madonna
of the Rocks, her smile swayed under the blue hood,

and when her fluted robe stilled, the smile stayed on her
dimpled porcelain. She saw, in the bowed man, the calm
common oval of prayer, the head's usual angle

over the pew of the dashboard. Her lifted palm,
small as a doll's from its cerulean mantle,
indicated that he had prayed enough to the lace

of foam round the cliff's altar, that now, if he wished,
he could lift his head, but he stayed in the same place,
the way a man will remain when Mass is finished,

not unclenching his hands or freeing one to cross
forehead, heart, and shoulders swiftly and then kneel
facing the altar. He bowed in endless remorse,

for her mercy at what he had done to Achille,
his brother. But his arc was over, for the course
of every comet is such. The fated crescent

was printed on the road by the scorching tires.
A salt tear ran down the porcelain cheek and it went
in one slow drop to the clenched knuckle that still gripped

the wheel. On the flecked sea, the uninterrupted
wind herded the long African combers, and whipped
the small flag of the island on its silver spearhead.

II

Drivers leant over the rail. One seized my luggage
off the porter's cart. The rest burst into patois,
with gestures of despair at the lost privilege

of driving me, then turned to other customers.
In the evening pastures horses grazed, their hides wet
with light that shot its lances over the combers.

I had the transport all to myself.
                                    "You all set?
Good. A good pal of mine died in that chariot
of his called the Comet."
                                    He turned in the front seat,

spinning the air with his free hand. I sat, sprawled out
in the back, discouraging talk, with my crossed feet.
"You never know when, eh? I was at the airport

that day. I see him take off like a rocket.
I always said that thing have too much horsepower.
And so said, so done. The same hotel, chief, correct?"

I saw the coastal villages receding as
the highway's tongue translated bush into forest,
the wild savannah into moderate pastures,

that other life going in its "change for the best,"
its peace paralyzed in a postcard, a concrete
future ahead of it all, in the cinder-blocks

of hotel development with the obsolete
craft of the carpenter, as I sensed, in the neat
marinas, the fisherman's phantom. Old oarlocks

and rusting fretsaw. My craft required the same
crouching care, the same crabbed, natural devotion
of the hand that stencilled a flowered window-frame

or planed an elegant canoe; its time was gone
with the spirit in the wood, as wood grew obsolete
and plasterers smoothed the blank page of white concrete.

I watched the afternoon sea. Didn't I want the poor
to stay in the same light so that I could transfix
them in amber, the afterglow of an empire,

preferring a shed of palm-thatch with tilted sticks
to that blue bus-stop? Didn't I prefer a road
from which tracks climbed into the thickening syntax

of colonial travellers, the measured prose I read
as a schoolboy? That cove, with its brown shallows
there, Praslin? That heron? Had they waited for me

to develop my craft? Why hallow that pretence
of preserving what they left, the hypocrisy
of loving them from hotels, a biscuit-tin fence

smothered in love-vines, scenes to which I was attached
as blindly as Plunkett with his remorseful research?
Art is History's nostalgia, it prefers a thatched

roof to a concrete factory, and the huge church
above a bleached village. The gap between the driver
and me increased when he said:

> "The place changing, eh?"

where an old rumshop had gone, but not that river
with its clogged shadows. *That* would make me a stranger.
"All to the good," he said. I said, "All to the good,"

then, "whoever they are," to myself. I caught his eyes
in the mirror. We were climbing out of Micoud.
Hadn't I made their poverty my paradise?

His back could have been Hector's, ferrying tourists
in the other direction home, the leopard seat
scratching their damp backs like the fur-covered armrests.

He had driven his burnt-out cargo, tired of sweat,
who longed for snow on the moon and didn't have to face
the heat of that sinking sun, who knew a climate

as monotonous as this one could only produce
from its unvarying vegetation flashes
of a primal insight like those red-pronged lilies

that shot from the verge, that their dried calabashes
of fake African masks for a fake Achilles
rattled with the seeds that came from other men's minds.

So let them think that. Who needed art in this place
where even the old women strode with stiff-backed spines,
and the fishermen had such adept thumbs, such grace

these people had, but what they envied most in them
was the calypso part, the Caribbean lilt
still in the shells of their ears, like the surf's rhythm,

until too much happiness was shadowed with guilt
like any Eden, and they sighed at the sign:
HEWANNORRA (Iounalao), the gold sea

flat as a credit-card, extending its line
to a beach that now looked just like everywhere else,
Greece or Hawaii. Now the goddamn souvenir

felt absurd, excessive. The painted gourds, the shells.
Their own faces as brown as gourds. Mine felt as strange
as those at the counter feeling their bodies change.

III

Change lay in our silence. We had come to that bend
where the trees are warped by wind, and the cliffs, raw,
shelve surely to foam.
                    "Is right here everything end,"

the driver said, and rammed open the transport door
on his side, then mine.
                    "Anyway, chief, the view nice."
I joined him at the gusting edge.
                    "His name was Hector."

The name was bent like the trees on the precipice
to point inland. In its echo a man-o'-war
screamed on the wind. The driver moved off for a piss,

then shouted over his shoulder:
                                        "A road-warrior.
He would drive like a madman when the power took.
He had a nice woman. Maybe he died for her."

For her and tourism, I thought. The driver shook
himself, zipping then hoisting his crotch.
                                        "Crazy, but
a gentle fellow anyway, with a very good brain."

Cut to a leopard galloping on a dry plain
across Serengeti. Cut to the spraying fans
drummed by a riderless stallion, its wild mane

scaring the Scamander. Cut to a woman's hands
clenched towards her mouth with no sound. Cut to the wheel
of a chariot's spiked hubcap. Cut to the face

of his muscling jaw, then flashback to Achille
hurling a red tin and a cutlass. Next, a vase
with a girl's hoarse whisper echoing "Omeros,"

as in a conch-shell. Cut to a shield of silver
rolling like a hubcap. Rewind, in slow motion,
myrmidons gathering by a village river

with lances for oars. Cut to the surpliced ocean
droning its missal. Cut. A crane hoisting a wreck.
A horse nosing the surf, then shuddering its neck.

He'd paid the penalty of giving up the sea
as graceless and as treacherous as it had seemed,
for the taxi-business; he was making money,

but all of that money was making him ashamed
of the long afternoons of shouting by the wharf
hustling passengers. He missed the uncertain sand

under his feet, he sighed for the trough of a wave,
and the jerk of the oar when it turned in his hand,
and the rose conch sunset with its low pelicans.

Castries was corrupting him with its roaring life,
its littered market, with too many transport vans
competing. Castries had been his common-law wife

who, like Helen, he had longed for from a distance,
and now he had both, but a frightening discontent
hollowed his face; to find that the sea was a love

he could never lose made every gesture violent:
ramming the side-door shut, raking the clutch. He drove
as if driven by furies, but furies paid the rent.

A man who cursed the sea had cursed his own mother.
Mer was both mother and sea. In his lost canoe
he had said his prayers. But now he was in another

kind of life that was changing him with his brand-new
stereo, its endless garages, where he could not
whip off his shirt, hearing the conch's summoning note.

Chapter XLVI

I

Hector was buried near the sea he had loved once.
Not too far from the shallows where he fought Achille
for a tin and Helen. He did not hear the sea-almond's

moan over the bay when Philoctete blew the shell,
nor the one drumbeat of a wave-thud, nor a sail
rattling to rest as its day's work was over,

and its mate, gauging depth, bent over the gunwale,
then wearily sounding the fathoms with an oar,
the same rite his shipmates would repeat soon enough

when it was their turn to lie quiet as Hector,
lowering a pitch-pine canoe in the earth's trough,
to sleep under the piled conchs, through every weather

on the violet-wreathed mound. Crouching for his friend to hear,
Achille whispered about their ancestral river,
and those things he would recognize when he got there,

his true home, forever and ever and ever,
forever, *compère*. Then Philoctete limped over
and rested his hand firmly on a shaking shoulder

to anchor his sorrow. Seven Seas and Helen
did not come nearer. Achille had carried an oar
to the church and propped it outside with the red tin.

Now his voice strengthened. He said: "Mate, this is your spear,"
and laid the oar slowly, the same way he had placed
the parallel oars in the hull of the gommier

the day the African swift and its shadow raced.
And this was the prayer that Achille could not utter:
"The spear that I give you, my friend, is only wood.

Vexation is past. I know how well you treat her.
You never know my admiration, when you stood
crossing the sun at the bow of the long canoe

with the plates of your chest like a shield; I would say
any enemy so was a compliment. 'Cause no
African ever hurled his wide seine at the bay

by which he was born with such beauty. You hear me? Men
did not know you like me. All right. Sleep good. Good night."
Achille moved Philoctete's hand, then he saw Helen

standing alone and veiled in the widowing light.
Then he reached down to the grave and lifted the tin
to her. Helen nodded. A wind blew out the sun.

I I

Pride set in Helen's face after this, like a stone
bracketed with Hector's name; her lips were incised
by its dates in parenthesis. She seemed more stern,

more ennobled by distance as she slowly crossed
the hot street of the village like a distant sail
on the horizon. Grief heightened her. When she smiled

it was with such distance that it was hard to tell
if she had heard your condolence. It was the child,
Ma Kilman told them, that made her more beautiful.

III

The rites of the island were simplified by its elements,
which changed places. The grooved sea was Achille's garden,
the ridged plot of rattling plantains carried their sense

of the sea, and Philoctete, on his height, often heard, in
a wind that suddenly churned the rage of deep gorges,
the leafy sound of far breakers plunging with smoke,

and for smoke there were the bonfires which the sun catches
on the blue heights at sunrise, doing the same work
as Philoctete clearing his plot, just as, at sunset,

smoke came from the glowing rim of the horizon as if
from his enamel pot. The woodsmoke smelt of a regret
that men cannot name. On the charred field, the massive

sawn trunks burnt slowly like towers, and the great
indigo dusk slowly plumed down, devouring the still leaves,
igniting the firefly huts, lifting the panicky egret

to beat its lagoon and shelve in the cage of the mangroves,
take in the spars of its sails, then with quick-pricking head
anchor itself shiftingly, and lift its question again.

At night, the island reversed its elements, the heron
of a quarter-moon floated from Hector's grave, rain
rose upwards from the sea, and the corrugated iron

of the sea glittered with nailheads. Ragged
plantains bent and stepped with their rustling powers
over the furrows of Philoctete's garden, a chorus of aged

ancestors and straw, and, rustling, surrounded every house
in the village with its back garden, with its rank midden
of rusted chamber pots, rotting nets, and the moon's cold basin.

They sounded, when they shook, after the moonlit meridian
of their crossing, like the night-surf; they gazed in
silence at the shadows of their lamplit children.

At Philoctete, groaning and soaking the flower on his shin
with hot sulphur, cleaning its edges with yellow Vaseline,
and, gripping his knee, squeezing rags from the basin.

At night, when yards are asleep, and the broken line
of the surf hisses like Philo, *"Bon Dieu, aie, waie,* my sin
is this sore?" the old plantains suffer and shine.

Chapter XLVII

I

Islands of bay leaves in the medicinal bath
of a cauldron, a sibylline cure. The citron
sprig of a lime-tree dividing the sky in half

dipped its divining rod. The white spray of the thorn,
which the swift bends lightly, waited for a black hand
to break it in bits and boil its leaves for the wound

from the pronged anchor rusting in clean bottom-sand.
Ma Kilman, in a black hat with its berried fringe,
eased herself sideways down the broken concrete step

of the rumshop's back door, closed it, and rammed the hinge
tight. The bolt caught a finger and with that her instep
arch twisted and she let out a soft Catholic

curse, then crossed herself. She closed the gate. The asphalt
sweated with the heat, the limp breadfruit leaves were thick
over the fence. Her spectacles swam in their sweat.

She plucked an armpit. The damn wig was badly made.
She was going to five o'clock Mass, to *la Messe*,
and sometimes she had to straighten it as she prayed

until the wafer dissolved her with tenderness,
the way a raindrop melts on the tongue of a breeze.
In the church's cool cave the sweat dried from her eyes.

She rolled down the elastic bands below the knees
of her swollen stockings. It was then that their vise
round her calves reminded her of Philoctete. Then,

numbering her beads, she began her own litany
of berries, Hail Mary marigolds that stiffen
their aureoles in the heights, mild anemone

and clear watercress, the sacred heart of Jesus
pierced like the anthurium, the thorns of logwood,
called the tree of life, the aloe good for seizures,

the hole in the daisy's palm, with its drying blood
that was the hole in the fisherman's shin since he was
pierced by a hook; there was the pale, roadside tisane

of her malarial childhood. There was this one
for easing a birth-breach, that one for a love-bath,
before the buds of green sugar-apples in the sun

ripened like her nipples in girlhood. But what path
led through nettles to the cure, the furious sibyl
couldn't remember. Mimosa winced from her fingers,

shutting like jalousies at some passing evil
when she reached for them. The smell of incense lingers
in her clothes. Inside, the candle-flames are erect

round the bier of the altar while she and her friends
old-talk on the steps, but the plant keeps its secret
when her memory reaches, shuttering in its fronds.

II

The dew had not yet dried on the white-ribbed awnings
and the nodding palanquins of umbrella yams
where the dark grove had not heat but early mornings

of perpetual freshness, in which the bearded arms
of a cedar held council. Between its gnarled toes
grew the reek of an unknown weed; its pronged flower

sprang like a buried anchor; its windborne odours
diverted the bee from its pollen, but its power,
rooted in bitterness, drew her bowed head by the nose

as a spike does a circling bull. To approach it
Ma Kilman lowered her head to one side and screened
the stench with a cologned handkerchief. The mulch it

was rooted in carried the smell, when it gangrened,
of Philoctete's cut. In her black dress, her berried
black hat, she climbed a goat-path up from the village,

past the stones with dried palms and conchs, where the buried
suffer the sun all day Sunday, while goats forage
the new wreaths. Once more she pulled at the itch in her

armpits, nearly dropping her purse. Then she climbed hard
up the rain-cracked path, the bay closing behind her
like a wound, and rested. Everything that echoed

repeated its outline: a goat's doddering bleat,
a hammer multiplying a roof, and, through the back yards,
a mother cursing a boy too nimble to beat.

Ma Kilman picked up her purse and sighed on upwards
to the thread of the smell, one arm behind her back,
passing the cactus, the thorn trees, and then the wood

appeared over her, thick green, the green almost black
as her dress in its shade, its border of flowers
flecking the pasture with spray. Then she staggered back

from the line of ants at her feet. She saw the course
they had kept behind her, following her from church,
signalling a language she could not recognize.

III

A swift had carried the strong seed in its stomach
centuries ago from its antipodal shore,
skimming the sea-troughs, outdarting ospreys, her luck

held to its shadow. She aimed to carry the cure
that precedes every wound; the reversible Bight
of Benin was her bow, her target the ringed haze

of a circling horizon. The star-grains at night
made her hungrier; the leafless sea with no house
for her weariness. Sometimes she dozed in her flight

for a swift's second, closing the seeds of her stare,
then ruddering straight. The dry sea-flakes whitened her
breast, her feathers thinned. Then, one dawn the day-star

rose slowly from the wrong place and it frightened her
because all the breakers were blowing from the wrong
east. She saw the horned island and uncurled her claws

with one frail cry, since swifts are not given to song,
and fluttered down to a beach, ejecting the seed
in grass near the sand. She nestled in dry seaweed.

In a year she was bleached bone. All of that motion
a pile of fragile ash from the fire of her will,
but the vine grew its own wings, out of the ocean

it climbed like the ants, the ancestors of Achille,
the women carrying coals after the dark door
slid over the hold. As the weed grew in odour

so did its strength at the damp root of the cedar,
where the flower was anchored at the mottled root
as a lizard crawled upwards, foot by sallow foot.

Chapter XLVIII

Under the thick leaves of the forest, there's a life
more intricate than ours, with our vows of love,
that seethes under the spider's veil on the wet leaf.

There's a race of beetles whose nature is to bleed
the very source that nourishes them, till the host
is a rattling carapace; slowly they proceed

to a fecund partner, mounting the dry one's ghost.
No, there is no such insect, but there are creatures
with two legs only, but with pincers in their eyes,

and arms that clinch and stroke us; they hang like leeches
on the greenest vines, from the veins of paradise.
And often, in the female, what may seem wilful

will seem like happiness, that spasmic ecstasy
which ejects the fatal acid, from which men fall
like a desiccated leaf; and this natural history

is not confined to the female of the species,
it all depends on who gains purchase, since the male,
like the dung-beetle storing up its dry feces,

can leave its exhausted mate hysterical, pale.
This is succession, it hides underneath a log,
it crawls on a shaken flower, and then both mates

embrace, and forgive; then the usual epilogue
occurs, where one lies weeping, which the other hates.
All I had gotten I deserved, I now saw this,

and though I had self-contempt for my own deep pain,
I lay drained in bed, like the same dry carapace
I had made of others, till my turn came again.

It could not lift the heavy agonies I felt
for the fatherless wanderings of my own sons,
but some sorrows are like stones, and they never melt,

though our tears rain and groove them, and the other ones,
the marriages dissolved like sand through the fingers,
the *per mea culpa* that had emptied all hope

from cupboards where some scent of happiness lingers
in camphor, in a lost hairpin crusted with soap;
the love I was good at seemed to have been only

the love of my craft and nature; yes, I was kind,
but with such certitude it made others lonely,
and with such bent industry it had made me blind.

It was a cry that called from the rock, some water
that the sea-swift crossed alone, and the calling stayed
like the hoarse echo in the conch; it called me from daughter

and son, it called me from my bed at dawn in darkness
like a fisherman walking towards the white noise
of paper, then in its hollow craft sets his oars.

It is what Achille learnt under the dark ceiling
of sea-grapes dripping with rain that puckered the sand:
that there is no error in love, of feeling

the wrong love for the wrong person. The still island
seasoned the wound with its salt; he scooped the bucket
and emptied the bilge with its leaves of manchineel,

thinking of the stitched, sutured wound that Philoctete
was given by the sea, but how the sea could heal
the wound also. And that was what Ma Kilman taught.

She glimpsed gods in the leaves, but, their features obscured
by the restless shade and light, those momentary
guardians, unlike the logwood thorns of her Lord,

or that golden host named for her mother, Mary,
thronging around her knees, with some soldiery crushed
by the weight of a different prayer, had lost their names

and, therefore, considerable presence. They had rushed
across an ocean, swifter than the swift, numerous
in loud migration as the African swallows

or bats that circle a cotton-tree at sunset
when their sight is strong and branches uphold the house
of heaven; so the deities swarmed in the thicket

of the grove, waiting to be known by name; but she
had never learnt them, though their sounds were within her,
subdued in the rivers of her blood. Erzulie,

Shango, and Ogun; their outlines fading, thinner
as belief in them thinned, so that all their power,
their roots, and their rituals were concentrated

in the whorled corolla of that stinking flower.
All the unburied gods, for three deep centuries dead,
but from whose lineage, as if her veins were their roots,

her arms ululated, uplifting the branches
of a tree carried across the Atlantic that shoots
fresh leaves as its dead trunk wallows on our beaches.

They were there. She called them. They had knotted the shouts
in her throat like a vine. They were the bats whose screeches
are shriller than what a dog hears. Ma Kilman heard

and saw them when their wings with crisscrossing stitches
blurred in the leaf-breaks, building a web overhead,
a net that entered her nerves, and her skin itches

as if flailed with a nettle. She foraged for some sign
of the stinging bush, and thrashed herself for the sin
of doubting their names before the cure could begin.

II

The wild, wire-haired, and generously featured
apotheosis of the caverned prophetess
began. Ma Kilman unpinned the black, red-berried

straw-hat with its false beads, lifted the press
of the henna wig, made of horsehair, from the mark
on her forehead. Carefully, she set both aside

on the coiled green follicles of moss in the dark
wood. Her hair sprung free as the moss. Ants scurried
through the wiry curls, barring, then passing each other

the same message with scribbling fingers and forehead
touching forehead. Ma Kilman bent hers forward,
and as her lips moved with the ants, her mossed skull heard

the ants talking the language of her great-grandmother,
the gossip of a distant market, and she understood,
the way we follow our thoughts without any language,

why the ants sent her this message to come to the wood
where the wound of the flower, its gangrene, its rage
festering for centuries, reeked with corrupted blood,

seeped the pustular drops instead of sunlit dew
into the skull, the brain of the earth, in the mind
ashamed of its flesh, its hair. On the varnished pew

of the church, she remembered the frantic messenger
that had paused, making desperate signs, its oars
lifted, but she had ignored the deaf-mute anger

of the insect signing a language that was not hers,
but now Ma Kilman, her hair wild, followed the vine
of the generations of silent black workers, their hands

passing stones so quickly against the white line
of breakers, with coal-baskets, with invisible sounds,
and the cries of the insects led her where she bowed

her bare head and unbuttoned the small bone buttons
of her church dress. Ma Kilman, in agony, bayed
up at the lights moving in the high leaves, like aeons,

like atoms, her dugs shifting like the sow's in a shift
of cheap satin. She rubbed dirt in her hair, she prayed
in the language of ants and her grandmother, to lift

the sore from its roots in Philoctete's rotting shin,
from the flower on his shin-blade, puckering inwards;
she scraped the earth with her nails, and the sun

put the clouds to its ears as her screech reeled backwards
to its beginning, from the black original cave
of the sibyl's mouth, her howl made the emerald lizard

lift one clawed leg, remembering the sound.
Philoctete shook himself up from the bed of his grave,
and felt the pain draining, as surf-flowers sink through sand.

III

See her there, my mother, my grandmother, my great-great-
grandmother. See the black ants of their sons,
their coal-carrying mothers. Feel the shame, the self-hate

draining from all our bodies in the exhausted sleeping
of a rumshop closed Sunday. There was no difference
between me and Philoctete. One wound gibbers in the weeping

mouth of the sibyl, the obeah-woman, in the swell
of the huge white satin belly, the dark gust that bent her
limbs till she was a tree of snakes, the spidery sibyl

hanging in a sack from the cave at Cumae, the obeah
that possessed her that the priests considered evil
in their white satin frocks, because ants had lent her

their language, the flower that withered on the floor
of moss smelt sweet and spread its antipodal odour
from the seed of the swift; now through a hot meadow

of unnamed flowers, a large woman in a red-berried
hat is walking. She comes down the broken brown road
past the first houses, past the sun-stricken yards, the bed

of a rivulet, past the crunching goats, where the buried
lie under the cement stones at whose base the moss
is evergreen, then the galvanized fences of rusted

tin-covers, as if she had stopped off after Mass
to gossip with neighbours, like ants at the end of a log,
or the end of a street. Where Seven Seas, and a dog

coiled in the dial's shade of the pharmacy,
closed for Sunday, senses her black, passing shape,
and the only sound is the hot, lazy drum of the sea.

Chapter XLIX

I

She bathed him in the brew of the root. The basin
was one of those cauldrons from the old sugar-mill,
with its charred pillars, rock pasture, and one grazing

horse, looking like helmets that have tumbled downhill
from an infantry charge. Children rang them with stones.
Wildflowers sprung in them when the dirt found a seam.

She had one in her back yard, close to the crotons,
agape in its crusted, agonized O: the scream
of centuries. She scraped its rusted scabs, she scoured

the mouth of the cauldron, then fed a crackling pyre
with palms and banana-trash. In the scream she poured
tin after kerosene tin, its base black from fire,

of seawater and sulphur. Into this she then fed
the bubbling root and leaves. She led Philoctete
to the gurgling lava. Trembling, he entered

his bath like a boy. The lime leaves leeched to his wet
knuckled spine like islands that cling to the basin
of the rusted Caribbean. An icy sweat

glazed his scalp, but he could feel the putrescent shin
drain in the seethe like sucked marrow, he felt it drag
the slime from his shame. She rammed him back to his place

as he tried climbing out with: "Not yet!" With a rag
sogged in a basin of ice she rubbed his squeezed face
the way boys enjoy their mother's ritual rage,

and as he surrendered to her, the foul flower
on his shin whitened and puckered, the corolla
closed its thorns like the sea-egg. What else did it cure?

II

The bow leapt back to the palm of the warrior.
The yoke of the wrong name lifted from his shoulders.
His muscles loosened like those of a brown river

that was dammed with silt, and then silkens its boulders
with refreshing strength. His ribs thudded like a horse
cantering on a beach that bursts into full gallop

while a boy yanks at its rein with terrified "Whoas!"
The white foam unlocked his coffles, his ribbed shallop
broke from its anchor, and the water, which he swirled

like a child, steered his brow into the right current,
as calm as *In God We Troust* to that other world,
and his flexed palm enclosed an oar with the ident-

ical closure of a mouth around its own name,
the way a sea-anemone closes slyly
into a secrecy many mistake for shame.

Centuries weigh down the head of the swamp-lily,
its tribal burden arches the sea-almond's spine,
in barracoon back yards the soul-smoke still passes,

but the wound has found her own cure. The soft days spin
the spittle of the spider in webbed glasses,
as she drenches the burning trash to its last flame,

and the embers steam and hiss to the schoolboys' cries
when he'd weep in the window for their tribal shame.
A shame for the loss of words, and a language tired

of accepting that loss, and then all accepted.
That was why the sea stank from the frothing urine
of surf, and fish-guts reeked from the government shed,

and why God pissed on the village for months of rain.
But now, quite clearly the tears trickled down his face
like rainwater down a cracked carafe from Choiseul,

as he stood like a boy in his bath with the first clay's
innocent prick! So she threw Adam a towel.
And the yard was Eden. And its light the first day's.

And I felt the wrong love leaving me where I stood
on the café balcony facing the small square
and the tower with its banyan. I heard my blood

echoing the lifted leaves of the hills, and fear
leaving them like the rain; I felt her voice draining
from mine. A drizzle passed, but the sprinkled asphalt,

since the rain was shining and the sun was raining,
dried quickly with the smell of a singeing iron,
and whipped up the wet in sheets. My eyes were so clear

that I counted the barrack-arches on the Morne,
and traced the gauze of fine rain towards Soufrière
and imagined it cooling the bubbling pits of

the Malebolge, and beading its volcanic ferns
with clear, sliding drops. The roofs glittered with that love
which loses the other; clearer when it returns.

The process, the proof of a self-healing island
whose every cove was a wound, from the sibyl's art
renewed my rain-washed eyes. I felt an elation

opening and closing the valves of my panelled heart
like a book or a butterfly. The drying roofs
glittered with an interior light like Lucia's

and my joy was pounding like a stallion's hooves
on a morning beach scattering the crabbed wrestlers
near Helen's wall to this thudding metre it loves.

Of course we had loved each other, but differently,
as we loved the island. My braceleted Circe
was gone, like the shining drizzle, far now, at sea,

but the Caribbean ringed me with infinite mercy
as it did the island. In her white pillared house
I looked down from the wrong height, not like Philoctete

limping among his yams and the yam flowers.
My love was common as dirt; brown sheep bayed at it,
as it sang an old hymn and scraped a yard with a broom,

a yard with a bunioned plum-tree and old tires
under the bunioned plum-tree. It was rusted from
heat like a galvanized roof, it writhed from blue fires

of garbage, hens pecked its eyes out, smoke made it cry
for a begging breadfruit, an old head-scarfed woman
in the bible of an open window, a boy

steered it like a bicycle rim; like an onion
it wept openly. In a shop, with its felt hat,
it smelt of old age. It was carrying Hector's child,

and taking a break from the heat outside, it sat
fanning its parted thighs, and whenever it smiled,
it smiled for the island. It looked out on a street

of small, fretwork uprights. It yelped when a mongrel
skittered from a transport. All night, it sucked the sweet
of an Extra-Strong moon till it melted. The smell

of asphalt drying from rain was the breeze that shone
on Philoctete's skin, opening her gate with its bell,
then turning to fit the hook, closing that question.

Chapter L

Latticework shadows diamonded the verandah,
crossing out plans for the Plunketts' cruise. Brochures. Dates.
"Time, time," swayed the brass bells of the allamanda.

"Cheap! Cheap!" the sparrows chirruped round the breakfast plates.
On their last trip home he'd been shaken by it all:
England cashing in on decayed gentility

like the sneering portraits in their three-star hotel,
its frock-coated porter's coin-eyed humility;
its corner-pub, The Rodney, with its copper bell,

sporting prints, and brown quiet where a pint of ale,
two bangers and mash made his fist a sea-diver
coming up with a fortune. "It's the Admiral

Rob-Me, all right," he told Maud. Much of the river
was quietly preserved like the area-railing
near Putney Boat-House, where garden-boxes in June

exploded with chrysanthemums; but the ailing
statues of lions wearied him. One afternoon,
he so badly missed shaking the paw of his tom

drowsing in the window-light like a regular
lion that he cried. The bombsites had become
cubes of blue glass and indifferent steel. Trafalgar

was all tourists and cameras and the red roar
of pillar-box buses. They would begin to argue
over menus in windows. But the worst horror

was in the voices. Caught on a traffic island,
waiting for the sea-green light, he began to hear
the surf of a dialect none would understand;

it coiled in his ear-shell with its tireless moan,
feet could not muffle it nor traffic round the Strand,
nor a Kensington crescent remote as the moon.

I I

After the voices faded, he heard his own voice
growing brazen in its key from the hotel stair,
one step above that with which he spoke to the boys

on the estate. He searched the eyes of the waiter
pouring breakfast coffee with a frightening rage
at the spoon-clicking silence. Ringing the porter,

his pitch kept wavering on the proper language
and the correct key—not a plea, but an order.
This tightened his jawline and increased his hatred.

He thought of Tumbly and Scott. They'd fought the same war,
but he limped with pride at being the walking wounded
in the class-struggle, in the hotel's high ranking,

its brass-buttons and tips, and he might have ended
that way, saluting taxis and crisply thanking
gentlemen. The Major waited till his rage

ebbed and, with his eyes shut, his hands behind his head,
was ready to go back home. Through their ersatz lace
came the surf of cars. The sailing curtains lifted.

Level-voiced London unnerved him. He found his excuse
in its self-rapt adoration. Steering around
lines patiently forming at drizzling bus-queues,

umbrellas politely revolving in its rain,
the cold, beaded faces in raincoats and parkas,
he shook off the old hallucination again,

from a spun umbrella, that they were back at war.
On wet summer afternoons that grew dark as
February, its gutters muttered in patois

in the indigo light that spelt a hurricane
or thunder over Marble Arch. What he missed was
the roar of his island's market, palm-fronds talking

to each other. It was one of the mysteries
of advancing age to like those tempestuous
gusts that hyphenated leaves on a railed walk, in-

stead of keeping things in place and their proper use.
He felt like a strolling statue, passing the *News
of the World*, and the Thames looked smaller to his eyes.

III

Maud could never sleep the length of those afternoons;
stretched out on the verandah in the chaise-longue, and
fanning with a palmetto, deep in her cushions,

she stopped to examine the maps along one hand.
Dennis was sprawled out upstairs in his khaki shirt.
In the hot breeze everything stirred like an omen.

She knew it was coming, but when? In the inert
pasture with its quiet trees? In the wide-open
bay? Was its message that rooster kicking up dirt

like a grave near her kitchen just behind the pen?
In a donkey's bray sawing the heat? It was not
visible, it was only cold sweat on her brow.

In the day's slow yawn before it swallowed the night?
In the mango's leaves, the square shade under a cow?
Whenever you want, dear God, once it is not now.

She found herself exhausted before it was night.
In the heat, the low biplane of a dragonfly
buzzed the reed-wilted pond, as its rings spread the white

languid dominion of the crowned water-lily;
from their straw nets the orange beaks of the ginger-
lilies gaped for rain. She knew that it was silly

but she heard them screeching with the ceaseless hunger
of fledglings. She watered them. She personified
everything these days, from the archaic elegance

of Queen Anne's lace to the gold, imperious pride
of the sunflower's revolving, lion's countenance.
She preferred gardens to empires. Now she was tired.

Chapter LI

I

He still enjoyed taking Maud to five o'clock Mass,
backing out of the garage with the dewy stars
sharp through black trees, the metal wet, and Maud shawled as

if it were Ireland. Downhill, torches of roosters
caught a hill's edge, and the Rover's beam would surprise
clumps of grey workmen going to their factories,

all waiting for the first transport down the highway
with thermoses and construction hats in a breeze
as nippy as early spring, the greying road empty,

until, one morning, screeching round the cold asphalt,
twin lights had challenged him with incredible speed,
blinding him, until they veered and their driver called:

"Move your ass, honky!"
                   They were lucky to be spared.
Plunkett carefully parked the Rover near a ditch.
Maud was shaking. He kept the lights on and got out.

"Where're you going?" she screamed.
                        "For that sonofabitch!"
Plunkett said in the old Army voice. The transport
had braked to a screeching stop where the workmen were

waiting, and some of them were already inside
when he walked up the greying road like a major
out to bring them some discipline. One of them said:

"Mi 'n'homme blanc-a ka venir, oui." Meaning: "Here comes
the white man."
                        The dawn was coming up like thunder
through the coconut palms. Bagpipes and kettledrums

were the only thing missing. Plunkett smiled under
his martial, pensioned moustaches.
                                        "HOLD ON!" he roared.
They froze like recruits. One with his boot in the door.

"TILL I TALK TO THE DRIVER NO ONE GETS ABOARD!"
The driver rammed his side open. It was Hector.
"Are you the bloody driver?" he asked him quietly,

close to his face. "Are you drunk? We were nearly killed!"
The engine was on.
                        "Very well, give me the key.
Come, come on, the key," as if to a sulking child,

snapping his fingers. "And furthermore, I resent
the expletive you used. I am not a honky.
A donkey perhaps, a jackass, but I haven't spent

damned near twenty years on this godforsaken rock
to be cursed like a tourist. Do you understand?"
All the workmen were now in the van. "What de fock!"

one yelled. "Fock da honky!" Hector held out one hand.
It was hard as a cedar's roots.
                                        "Pardon, Major,
I didn't know it was you." It was only then

that Plunkett recognized the ivory smile. Hector,
of course, of course; he had been one of the fishermen
and had given up his canoe for this taxi. More

business. He steered the conversation to Helen
cunningly and asked if she was happy. Morning
wickered the palms' shadows on the warming asphalt.

He shook Hector's hand again, but with a warning
about his new responsibility.
                              "My fault,"
he said to Maud, turning the key in the engine.

                              I I

He dropped her off at the door of the cathedral
among other black-shawled women. The empty square
with rusty railings guarding the Memorial

still shone with the dew and its grass-green benches were
glazed with it. The fountain had uttered its last sigh.
The sidewalks were empty. He could park anywhere.

He parked the Rover in front of the library
with its Georgian trim and walked to the harbour.
Alone, down Bridge Street, he caught the smell of the sea

as the sunlight suddenly heightened the mutter
of Mass from the cathedral, and the balcony
uprights under which he passed rippling like water

or the dead fountain once. One sunrise in Lisbon,
walking along its empty wharves, he had wondered
where in this world he and his new wife could settle

to find some peace. At the Customs gate the old guard
let him in, unlocking it. He saw the metal
dazzle of the sea between rusty containers,

then the blue port itself, and on the opposite
headland the arches of Married Women's Quarters
and the old Officers' Mess as its hill was hit

by a salvo of light. He could hear the chuckle
of water under the hulls of island schooners,
and one still had a bulb on its binnacle

in spite of the sunshine. He strolled. His hunger was
pierced by the smell of coffee. He was repeating
with every step of his forked shadow the same pace

as the midshipman, centuries ago, reading
the italics of Dutch ships by moonlight. Now peace
swayed the creaking hulls of the schooners. His favourite

was an old freighter welded to the wharf by rust
and sunsets. He felt a deep tenderness for it,
that it went nowhere at all, grimed with coal-dust

from the back of the market, hung with old tires
as if it had had enough of the world. It once
had great plans for leaving, but after a few tries

it had grown attached to the helmeted capstans
to which it was moored and the light-surprising walls
of its retirement. Now, in their rising leaven,

clouds plump as dough grew fragrant as the long ovals
of crusting bread drawn out of a Creole oven
by spatulas longer than oars. The sunlight stuck

to his cheek, then ran down like salt butter
in the mouths of the loaves. Hunger gnawed his stomach
as he marched back to the gate. It was shut, but the

guard opened it again for him. He had to make
the bakery before they went, the wicker-woven
baskets emptied quickly; sometimes they'd be gone

before he and Maud got there. His Bread of Heaven
laced with salt butter, his private communion.
She was at the church door. He honked, hurrying her in.

III

Maud held the warm bag against her stomach and she
slapped his hand when it fumbled towards the package
of pointed loaves. "Pig." She smiled and stung his raw knee

with a slap, turning away in pretended rage
when he squeezed her thigh. "Dennis! I've just come from
church! Here. Why don't you squeeze one of these tits instead?"

By the time they crossed the wickered road to the farm
he had devoured two loaves of the fragrant bread
sunlit by the butter which he always carried.

Despite that morning's near-accident, the old Rover
sailed under the surf of threshing palms and his heart
hummed like its old engine, his wanderings over,

like the freighter rusting on its capstans. The heat
was wide now and the shadows blacker in the rows
of Maud's garden beds. Their fragrance did not draw her.

259

She smelt mortality in the oleanders
as well as the orchids; in the funeral-parlour
reek of stale water in vases. She went upstairs.

She didn't garden that morning. Sick of flowers.
Their common example of bodily decay,
from the brown old age of bridal magnolias

to the sunflower's empire that lasted a day.
By Bendemeer's stream. Nature had not betrayed her,
she smiled, lying in her bed. On the sun-streaked floor

the sunflower's dish, tracking the sun like radar,
altered the jalousies' shadows till they meant more
than the rays they let in. The gold wheel frightened her.

Chapter LII

I

The morning Maud died he sat in the bay window,
watching the angel-hair blow gently from her face.
That wax rose pillowed there was his crown and wonder,

a breeze lifting the curtains like her bridal lace.
Seashells. Seychelles. The empire of cancer spread
across the wrinkled sheets. Loosened from their ribbon,

his fleet of letters sailed their mahogany bed
close to a Macaulay and a calf-bound Gibbon,
an empire's bookends. His locket and his queen,

her golden knot his sovereign, and the covered keys
of the shawled piano she'd never play again.
She was his orb and sceptre, the shire of his peace,

the hedges aisling England, lanes ending in spires,
rooks that lift and scatter from oaks threshing like seas,
the black notes of sparrows on telegraph wires,

all these were in his letters, in the small brass-barred
chest next to her fingers, his voice was in each word.
She had been reading them in their carved double-bed.

That broke his grief. The Major stood, then staggered
to clutch the linen, burying his face inside her.
He rubbed their names against her stomach. "Maud, Maud,

it's Dennis, love, Maud." Then he stretched beside her,
as if they were statues on a stone tomb, so still
he heard the groan of a sun-expanded board

on the hot verandah, and from the roofs downhill
a bucket rattling for water, then the dry cardboard
rattle of breadfruit leaves on the bay-window sill.

II

Provinces, Protectorates, Colonies, Dominions,
Governors-General, black Knights, ostrich-plumed Viceroys,
deserts, jungles, hill-stations, all an empire's zones,

lay spilled from a small tea-chest; felt-footed houseboys
on fern-soft verandahs, hearty Toby-jugged Chiefs
of Police, Girl-Guide Commissioners, Secretaries,

poppies on cenotaphs, green-spined Remembrance wreaths,
cornets, kettledrums, gum-chewing dromedaries
under Lawrence, parasols, palm-striped pavilions,

dhows and feluccas, native-draped paddle-ferries
on tea-brown rivers, statue-rehearsing lions,
sandstorms seaming their eyes, horizontal monsoons,

rank odour of a sea-chest, mimosa memories
touched by a finger, lead soldiers, clopping Dragoons.
Breadfruit hands on a wall. The statues close their eyes.

Mosquito nets, palm-fronds, scrolled Royal Carriages,
dacoits, gun-bearers, snarling apes on Gibraltar,
sermons to sweat-soaked kerchiefs, the Rock of Ages

pumped by a Zouave band, lilies light the altar,
soldiers and doxies by a splashing esplanade,
waves turning their sheet music, the yellowing teeth

of the parlour piano, *Airs from Erin* played
to the whistling kettle, and on the teapot's head
the cozy's bearskin shako, biscuits break with grief,

gold-braid laburnums, lilac whiff of lavender,
columned poplars marching to Mafeking's relief.
Naughty seaside cards, the sepia surrender

of Gordon on the mantel, the steps of Khartoum,
The World's Classics condensed, Clive as brown as India,
bathers in Benares, an empire in costume.

His will be done, O Maud, His kingdom come,
as the sunflower turns, and the white eyes widen
in the ebony faces, the sloe-eyes, the bent smoke

where a pig totters across a village midden
over the sunset's shambles, Rangoon to Malta,
the regimental button of the evening star.

Solace of laudanum, menstrual cramps, the runnings,
tinkles in the jordan, at dusk the zebra shade
of louvres on the quilt, the maps spread their warnings

and the tribal odour of the second chambermaid.
And every fortnight, ten sharp on Sunday mornings,
shouts and wheeling patterns from our Cadet Brigade.

All spilt from a tea-chest, a studded souvenir,
props for an opera, Victoria Regina,
for a bolster-plump Queen the pillbox sentries stamp,

piss, straw and saddle-soap, heaume and crimson feather,
post-red double-deckers, spit-and-polished leather,
and iron dolphins leaping round an Embankment lamp.

III

There was Plunkett in my father, much as there was
my mother in Maud. Not just the morning-glories
or our own verandah's lilac bougainvilleas,

or the splayed hands of grape-leaves, of classic stories
on the barber's wooden shelf, the closest, of course,
was Helen's, but there in that khaki Ulysses

there was a changing shadow of Telemachus
in me, in his absent war, and an empire's guilt
stitched in the one pattern of Maud's fabulous quilt.

Chapter LIII

I

The Major stood straight as a mast without a sail
in the wooden waves of the pews. I turned my head
slowly, as we do at funerals, and saw the veil

that netted Helen's beauty. Then I tried to read
from the gilt hymnal with its ribbon, but felt the mesh
of her veil brushing my nape, and its black hairs stirred

with the legend behind my back, the smoke made flesh,
the phantom singed by a beach-fire. All I had heard
flamed in that look, galleys drowned in its wake.

This was the seduction of quicksand, my deep fear
of vertiginous irises that could not help their work
any more than the earth's fascination with fire

as it left the earth. An amen enclosed a hymn
and Plunkett's amen steadied the wavering choir
in the echoing stone. Fans, like moths, stirred the air.

And in that gap before the Father's injunction,
a smooth black priest with a smoother voice that pleased him
more than his listeners in its serene unction,

I felt the chasm that widened at Glen-da-Lough,
deep as a daisied trench, over the quilted bier,
the disenfranchisement no hyphenating rook

could connect between two religions, the one here
and that of our chapel. I turned around to look
at the black faces seized by faith and heard the whirr

of larches turning their missals, the Xeroxed sheets
that the Major had asked the priest to use in her
memory, for the midshipman, and the war's fading fleets.

I recognized Achille. He stood next to Philoctete
in a rusted black suit, his eyes anchored to the pew;
then he lifted them and I saw that the eyes were wet

as those of a boy, and my eyes were watering too.
Why should he be here, why should they have come at all,
none of them following the words, but he had such grace

that I couldn't bear it. I could leave the funeral,
but his wet ebony mask and her fishnetted face
were shrouded with Hector's death. Could he, in that small

suit too tight at the shoulders, who shovelled the pens
in the rain at Plunkett's, love him? Where was it from,
this charity of soul, more piercing than Helen's

beauty? runnelling his face like the road to the farm?
We sang behind Plunkett, and I saw Achille perspire
over the words, his lips following after the sound.

II

I knew little about Maud Plunkett. I knew I was here
because the Major had trained us all as cadets.
What I shared with his wife we shared as gardeners.

I had wanted large green words to lie waxen on
the page's skin, floating but rooted in its lymph as
her lilies in the pond's cool mud, every ivory prong

spreading the Japanese peace of *Les Nympheas*
in the tongue-still noon, the heat, where a wooden bridge
with narrow planks arched over the calligraphic

bamboo, their reflections rewritten when a midge
wrinkled the smoothness, and from them, the clear concentric
rings from a pebble, from the right noun on a page.

I was both there and not there. I was attending
the funeral of a character I'd created;
the fiction of her life needed a good ending

as much as mine; that night by the tasselled shade
with its oblong halo over her bowed hair sewing,
I had looked up from the green baize with the Major's

face from the ornate desk to see light going
from her image, and that image was my mother's,
whose death would be real, real as our knowing.

Join, interchangeable phantoms, expected pain
moves me towards ghosts, through this page's scrim,
and the ghosts I will make of you with my scratching pen,

like a needle piercing the ring's embroidery
with a swift's beak, or where, like a nib from the rim
of an inkwell, a martin flickers a wing dry.

Plunkett's falsetto soared like a black frigate-bird,
and shifted to a bass-cannon from his wattled throat,
Achille lowered his head for the way it circled

high over our pews, and I heard the brass bugle-note
of his khaki orders as we circled the Parade Ground,
and then the hymn ended. We watched the Major lift

his wife's coffin hung with orchids, many she had found
in the blue smoke of Saltibus. Then Achille saw the swift
pinned to the orchids, but it was the image of a swift

which Maud had sewn into the silk draping her bier,
and not only the African swift but all the horned island's
birds, bitterns and herons, silently screeching there.

III

When Plunkett passed, Achille looked at his red hands,
and the Major widened his eyes at him and Philoctete,
and nodded at Helen, who turned her black veil away,

and he saw her head shaking under the covering net.
Then the big shots passed, and every brown dignitary,
some with medals and ribbons, gave them a short smile

of gracious detachment, but with no special surprise
at their devotion. Achille waited till the aisle
emptied, the gilt missals were replaced in their pews,

then stood outside at the church door as the filled hearse
opened for the orchids and the bird-choked tapestry
straightened. I saw Helen, in that slow walk of hers,

come and lean next to him. She lifted the eyed veil,
and said: "I coming home." Then he and Philoctete
walked with her to the transports near the Coal Market.

Chapter LIV

I saw him at the bank next day, moustache bristling,
white, irascible cockatoo hair, the red hands,
the mouth puckered forward, inaudibly whistling.

The man behind me said: "Collecting insurance.
So fast, boy?"
            I turned and said, "Dat ain't so funny."
He stood behind the banana-farmers in line.

They smelt of wet earth, they smelt green as their money.
I thought of his own deposits, stinking of swine,
as he stood in his flaccid shorts, his khaki shirt

carrying a black armband, and I saw that he was
one with the farmers, transplanted to the rich dirt
of their valleys, a ginger-lily from the moss

of Troumasse River, a white, red-knuckled heron
in the reeds, who never wanted the privilege
that peasants, from habit, paid to his complexion.

He stood his turn in the queue, then at the cage
he bent to the teller's bars, and I heard the old voice
hoarsely requesting his rolls of coins in silver,

and the voice carried the old bugle-note that as boys
had racked us in line as cadets. I felt that shiver
of fear we all knew. His shout could carry over

the heights of Saltibus to the cliffs of D'Elles Soeurs,
the khaki slopes of D'Elles Soeurs to LaFargue River.
Then he passed my queue, as if it were Inspection.

"Our wanderer's home, is he?"
                                        I said: "For a while, sir,"
too crisply, mentally snapping to attention,
thumbs along trousers' seam, picking up his accent

from a khaki order.
                    "Been travellin' a bit, what?"
I forgot the melody of my own accent,
but I knew I'd caught him, and he knew he'd been caught,

caught out in the class-war. It stirred my contempt.
He knew the "what?" was a farce, I knew it was not
officer-quality, a strutting R.S.M.,

Regimental Sarn't Major Plunkett, Retired.
Not real colonial gentry, but spoke like
them from the height of his pig-farm, but I felt as tired

as he looked. Still, he'd led us in Kipling's requiem.
"Been doin' a spot of writing meself. Research."
The "meself" his accommodation. "P'raps you've 'eard . . .

the old queen," shrugging. I said I'd been at the church.
"Ah! Were you? These things. Eyes tend to get very blurred.
So sorry I missed you. Bit of an artist, too,

was old Maud. You must come up. I'll show you a quilt
she embroidered for years. Birds and things. Mustn't keep you."
O Christ! I swore, I'm tired of their fucking guilt,

and our fucking envy! War invented the queue,
and he taught that Discipline formed its own beauty
in the rhyming steps of the college Cadet Force,

that though crowds mimicked his strut, it was his duty
to make us all gentlemen if not officers.
"Nice to see you, sir," said my old Sergeant Major,

and my eyes blurred. Then he paused at the white glare of
the street outside, and left, as the guard closed the door,
the wound of a language I'd no wish to remove.

I I

I remembered that morning when Plunkett and I,
compelled by her diffident saunter up the beach,
sought grounds for her arrogance. He in the khaki

grass round the redoubt, I in the native speech
of its shallows; like enemy ships of the line,
we crossed on a parallel; he had been convinced

that his course was right; I despised any design
that kept to a chart, that calculated the winds.
My inspiration was impulse, but the Major's zeal

to make her the pride of the Battle of the Saints,
her yellow dress on its flagship, was an ideal
no different from mine. Plunkett, in his innocence,

had tried to change History to a metaphor,
in the name of a housemaid; I, in self-defence,
altered her opposite. Yet it was all for her.

Except we had used two opposing stratagems
in praise of her and the island; cannonballs rolled
in the fort grass were not from Olympian games,

nor the wine-bottle, crusted with its fool's gold,
from the sunken *Ville de Paris*, legendary
emblems; nor all their names the forced coincidence

we had made them. There, in her head of ebony,
there was no real need for the historian's
remorse, nor for literature's. Why not see Helen

as the sun saw her, with no Homeric shadow,
swinging her plastic sandals on that beach alone,
as fresh as the sea-wind? Why make the smoke a door?

III

All that Greek manure under the green bananas,
under the indigo hills, the rain-rutted road,
the galvanized village, the myth of rustic manners,

glazed by the transparent page of what I had read.
What I had read and rewritten till literature
was guilty as History. When would the sails drop

from my eyes, when would I not hear the Trojan War
in two fishermen cursing in Ma Kilman's shop?
When would my head shake off its echoes like a horse

shaking off a wreath of flies? When would it stop,
the echo in the throat, insisting, "Omeros";
when would I enter that light beyond metaphor?

But it was mine to make what I wanted of it, or
what I thought was wanted. A cool wood off the road,
a hut closed like a wound, and the sound of a river

coming through the trees on a country Saturday,
with no one in the dry front yard, the still leaves,
the yard, the shade of a breadfruit tree on the door,

then the track from which a man's figure emerges,
then a girl carrying laundry, the road-smell like loaves,
the yellow-dressed butterflies in the grass marges.

Chapter LV

I

Through the year, pain came and went. Then came Christmas,
everything right and exact, everything correct,
the golden pillars of Scotch, red sorrel, sea-moss,

the hunger of happiness spread through Philoctete
like a smooth white tablecloth, everything in place,
the plastic domes of hot dishes frosting with dew,

gravy-boats anchored on patterns of doilied lace
withdrawn from camphored cupboards, the napkin holder
of yellow bone, the cutlery flashing in light

after a year in the drawer, shoulder to shoulder
the small army of uncorked wines and the corked-too-tight
explosives of ginger-beer, the ham pierced with cloves,

a crusted roast huge as a thigh, black pudding, souse,
the glazed cornmeal pies sweating in banana leaves,
and a smell of forgiveness drifting from each house

with the smell of varnish, and a peace that drifted
out to the empty beach; that brimmed in the eyes of
wineglasses, his heart bubbling when she lifted

the steaming shield from the rice. "Ah, Philosophe!"
he said to himself from the depth of gratitude,
"you cannot say life not good, or people not kind,"

as Ma Kilman sipped her sauce from the ladling wood
and pronounced, "It good," to both the one who was blind
and the healed one, in her generous widowhood.

The day after Christmas Achille rose excited
by the half-dark. A stale cock crew. Grass grew lighter
in the pastures. Moon-basins flashed in the riverbed.

Today he was not the usual kingfish-fighter
but a muscular woman, a scarf round his head.
Today was the day of fifes, the prattling skin

of the goat-drums, the day of dry gourds, of brass bells
round his ankles, not chains from the Bight of Benin
but those fastened by himself. He was someone else

today, a warrior-woman, fierce and benign.
Today he was African, his own epitaph,
his own resurrection. Today people would laugh

at what they had lost in the *paille-banane* dancers;
today was the day when they wore the calabash
with its marks; today the rustling banana-trash

would whirl with spinning Philoctete, the cancer's
anemone gone from his shin; the balancer's
day on the bamboo poles and the stilt-strider's height

floating past balconies, past the fretwork mansards;
today was the children's terror and their delight,
running up the street and hiding in people's yards.

Achille walked out into the blinding emptiness
of the shut village. He strode like a prizefighter
on Boxing Day, carrying Helen's yellow dress,

and the towel that matched it draped over his head,
the Lifebuoy soap in a dish swallowed by his hand
to wash off the love-sweat with Helen. By the shed

of the fishermen's depot a trough in the sand
held the public standpipe with its brass-knuckled fist.
The shower was a trickle. First Achille lathered

his skull white as Seven Seas's hair, then pulled the waist
of the trunks to forage his crotch. Then he rolled dirt
from back of the ankles with a hard-pressing wrist,

then rubbed one heel where the thorn-vine had left its hurt.
Then he opened the shower full out and let it drum
the streaming soap past his eyes, groping to close it.

"You smell like a flower," he teased himself. "How come?"
Next he unfrayed the soap-dried knots in his armpit,
and spray flew from his hair to the quick-picking comb.

The village was hung over. The sun slept in the street
like a dog, with no traffic. He shook Philo's gate.
The sufferer was cured now. He walked very straight.

Those elbows like anchors, those huge cannonball fists
wriggled through the armholes of the tight lemon dress.
Helen helped him stuff the rags and align his breasts.

At first she had laughed, but then, with firm tenderness,
Achille explained that he and Philo had done this
every Boxing Day, and not because of Christmas,

but for something older; something that he had seen
in Africa, when his name had followed a swift,
where he had been his own father and his own son.

The sail of her bellying stomach seemed to him
to bear not only the curved child sailing in her
but Hector's mound, and her hoarse, labouring rhythm

was a delivering wave. There, in miniature,
the world was globed like a fruit, since its texture is
both acid and sweet like a golden *pomme-Cythère*,

the apple of Venus, and the *Ville de Paris*
that he had dived for once, in search of a treasure
that was kneeling right there, that had always been his.

She did not laugh anymore, but she helped him lift
the bamboo frame with its ribbons and spread them out
from the frame, and everything she did was serious.

She knelt at his feet and hooked the bells to the skirt.
Small circular mirrors necklaced the split bodice
that was too small for his chest, and their flashing lights

multiplied her face with the tears in their own eyes.
She lifted the mitre, its panes like Easter kites,
and with this she fitted him. He straightened its spire

with his huge hands and their rope-furrowed calluses,
then he took up the wand and stood there in the mirror
of her pride and her butterfly-quiet kisses.

He was resinous and frightening. He smelt like trees
on a ridge at sunrise, like unswaying cedars;
then he set out for the hot road towards Castries,

the square already filling with tables. Buses
passed him with screaming children and in their cries
was the ocean's distance over three centuries.

III

Their small troupe stood in the hot street. Three musicians,
fife, chac-chac, and drummer and the androgynous
warriors, Philo and Achille. *Un! Deux! Trois!* The dance

began with Philo as its pivot, to the noise
of dry leaves scraping asphalt, the banana-trash
levitating him slowly as the roofs spun round

the dip and swivel of the head, a calabash
masking the agonized face, as Achille drummed the ground
with quick-stuttering heels, stopped. And then he stood straight.

Now he strode with the wand and the fluttering mitre
until he had walked to the far end of the street.
There he spun. Then, knee passing knee, he stepped lighter

than a woman with her skirt lifted high crossing
the stones of a stream when the light is small mirrors,
with the absurd strength of his calves and his tossing

neck, which shook out the mitre like a lion's mane,
with a long running leap, then a spin, while he held
the shaft low, like a rod divining. All the pain

re-entered Philoctete, of the hacked yams, the hold
closing over their heads, the bolt-closing iron,
over eyes that never saw the light of this world,

their memory still there although all the pain was gone.
He swallowed his nausea, and spun his arms faster,
like a goblet on a potter's wheel, its brown blur

soothed by his palms, as the bamboo fifes grew shriller
to the slitted eyes of the fifers. The drummer's wrists
whirred like a hummingbird's wings, and, to Achille, the

faster they flew, the more he remembered, blent
to his rite; then suddenly the music ceased.
The crowd clapped, and Achille, with great arrogance, sent

Philoctete to bow and pick up the coins on the street
glittering like fish-scales. He let the runnels of sweat
dry on his face. Philoctete sat down. Then he wept.

BOOK SEVEN

Chapter LVI

I

One sunrise I walked out onto the balcony
of my white hotel. The beach was already swept,
and in the clear grooves of the January sea

there was only one coconut shell, but it kept
nodding in my direction as a swimmer might
with sun in his irises, or a driftwood log,

or a plaster head, foaming. It changed shapes in light
according to each clouding thought. A khaki dog
came racing its faster shadow on the clean sand,

then stopped, yapping at the shell, not wetting its paws,
backing off from the claws of surf that made the sound
of a cat hissing; then it faked an interest

in a crab-hole and worried it. If that thing was
a coconut, why didn't it drift with the crest
of the slow-breathing swell? Then, as if from a vase,

or a girl's throat, I heard a moan from the village
of a blowing conch, and I saw the first canoe
on the horizon's glittering scales. The old age

of the wrinkled sea was in that moan, and I knew
that the floating head had drifted here. The mirrors
of the sky were clouded, and I heard my own voice

correcting his name, as the surf hissed: "Omeros."
The moment I named it, the marble head arose,
fringed with its surf curls and beard, the hollow shoulders

of a man waist-high in water with an old leather
goatskin or a plastic bag, pricking the dog's ears,
making it whine with joy. Then, suddenly, the weather

darkened, and it darkened the forked, slow-wading wood
until it was black, and the shallows in that second
changed to another dialect as Seven Seas stood

in the white foam manacling his heels. He beckoned,
that is, the arm of that log brought in by the tide,
then the cloud passed, and the white head glared, almond-eyed

in her white studio with its foam-scalloped beard
a winter ago, then it called to the khaki dog
that still backed off from the surf, yet now what appeared

changed again to its shadow, then a driftwood log
that halted and beckoned, moving to the foam's swell,
one elbow lifted, calling me from the hotel.

They kept shifting shapes, or the shapes metamorphosed
in the worried water; no sooner was the head
of the blind plaster-bust clear than its brow was crossed

by a mantling cloud and its visage reappeared
with ebony hardness, skull and beard like cotton,
its nose like a wedge; no sooner I saw the one

than the other changed and the first was forgotten
as the sand forgets a shadow in widening sun,
their bleached almond seeds their only thing in common.

So one changed from marble with a dripping chiton
in the early morning on that harp-wired sand
to a foam-headed fisherman in his white, torn

undershirt, but both of them had the look of men
whose skins are preserved in salt, whose accents were born
from guttural shoal, whose vision was wide as rain

sweeping over the sand, clouding the hills in gauze.
I came down to the beach. In its pointed direction,
the dog raced, passing the daisy-prints of its paws.

II

Up a steep path where even goats are careful,
the path that Philoctete took past the foaming cove,
the blind stone led me, my heart thudding and fearful

that it would burst like the sea in a drumming cave.
It was a cape that I knew, tree-bent and breezy,
no wanderer could have chosen a better grave.

If this was where it ended, the end was easy—
to give back the borrowed breath the joy that it gave,
with the sea exulting, the wind so wild with love.

His stubble chin jerked seaward, and the empty eyes
were filled with them, with the colour of the blue day;
so a swift will dart its beak just before it flies

towards its horizon, hazed Greece or Africa.
I could hear the crumpling parchment of the sea in
the wind's hand, a silence without emphasis,

but I saw no shadow underline my being;
I could see through my own palm with every crease
and every line transparent since I was seeing

the light of St. Lucia at last through her own eyes,
her blindness, her inward vision as revealing
as his, because a closing darkness brightens love,

and I felt every wound pass. I saw the healing
thorns of dry cactus drop to the dirt, and the grove
where the sibyl swayed. I thought of all my travelling.

III

"I saw you in London," I said, "sunning on the steps
of St. Martin-in-the-Fields, your dog-eared manuscript
clutched to your heaving chest. The queues at the bus-stops

smiled at your seaman's shuffle, and a curate kicked
you until you waddled down to the summery Thames."
"That's because I'm a heathen. They don't know my age.

Even the nightingales have forgotten their names.
The goat declines, head down, with these rocks for a stage
bare of tragedy. The Aegean's chimera

is a camera, you get my drift, a drifter
is the hero of my book."
                           "I never read it,"
I said. "Not all the way through."
                                     The lift of the

arching eyebrows paralyzed me like Medusa's
shield, and I turned cold the moment I had said it.
"Those gods with hyphens, like Hollywood producers,"

I heard my mouth babbling as ice glazed over my chest.
"The gods and the demi-gods aren't much use to us."
"Forget the gods," Omeros growled, "and read the rest."

Then there was the silence any injured author
knows, broken by the outcry of a frigate-bird,
as we both stared at the blue dividing water,

and in that gulf, I muttered, "I have always heard
your voice in that sea, master, it was the same song
of the desert shaman, and when I was a boy

your name was as wide as a bay, as I walked along
the curled brow of the surf; the word 'Homer' meant joy,
joy in battle, in work, in death, then the numbered peace

of the surf's benedictions, it rose in the cedars,
in the *lauriers-cannelles*, pages of rustling trees.
Master, I was the freshest of all your readers."

"Ready?"
          I nodded. We descended the goat-track,
down to the chumbling cove with its crescent beach,
and the old goat, skipping, shouted over his back:

"Who gave you my proper name in the ancient speech
of the islands?"
                    "A girl."
                                   We climbed down in silence.
"A Greek girl?"
                    "Who else?"
                                        "From what city? Do you know?"

"No. I forget."
                    "Thebes? Athens?"
                                             "Yeah. Could be Athens,"
I said, stumbling. "What difference does it make now?"
That stopped the old goat in his tracks. He turned:
                                                  "What differenc

None, maybe, to you, but a girl . . . that's very nice.
Her image rises out of every battle's noise.
A girl smells better than a book. I remember Helen's

smell. The sun on her flesh. The light's coins on my eyes.
That ten years' war was nothing, an epic's excuse.
Did you, you know, do it often?" Then his head tossed

at a horizon whose smile was as sad as his.
I saw in its empty line a love that was lost.
"Often," I lied. He said,
                              "Are they still fighting wars?"

I saw a coming rain hazing his pupils.
"Not over beauty," I answered. "Or a girl's love."
"Love is good, but the love of your own people is

greater."
              "Yes," I said. "That's why I walk behind you.
Your name in her throat's white vase sent me to find you."
"Good. A girl smells better than the world's libraries."

Chapter LVII

At the edge of the shallows was a black canoe
stayed by a grizzled oarsman, his white chin stubbled
as a dry sea-urchin's; but still I did not know

why, wading aboard, I felt such an untroubled
weightlessness, or why the ferryman held the prow,
except it was for that marble freight whose shadow

now sat amidships. The marble shaded its eyes
with one palm and shouted: "Home!" and the startled dog
scuttled into an almond grove. I heard the oars

clicking their teeth, but no wake followed the pirogue,
and the oarsman seemed to stare through me to the shore's
dividing line, as each stroke diminished its trees.

We followed the hotel's shoreline between bathers
whose bodies the oars passed through: lovers, families,
without dividing them yet. No one noticed us

or thought of that shadow wobbling underwater
that sharked towards them, breaking the sun-wired mesh,
or stared at our strange crew; it was only after

our current reached them that they stood hugging their flesh.
Then the oarsman smiled. The island filed past my eyes,
the hills that I knew, a road. I felt them going

for good round the point; then we were passing Castries,
the wharf where my father stood. The wharf was rowing
farther away from me till the white liner stuck

to the green harbour was no bigger than a toy,
as Seven Seas watched me with each receding stroke.
And my cheeks were salt with tears, but those of a boy,

and he saw how deeply I had loved the island.
Perhaps the oarsman knew this, but I didn't know.
Then I saw the ebony of his lifted hand.

And Omeros nodded: "We will both praise it now."
But I could not before him. My tongue was a stone
at the bottom of the sea, my mouth a parted conch

from which nothing sounded, and then I heard his own
Greek calypso coming from the marble trunk,
widening the sea with a blind man's anger:

"In the mist of the sea there is a horned island
with deep green harbours where the Greek ships anchor"
and the waves were swaying to the stroke of his hand,

as I heard my own thin voice riding on his praise
the way a swift follows a crest, leaving its shore:
"It was a place of light with luminous valleys

under thunderous clouds. A Genoan wanderer
saying the beads of the Antilles named the place
for a blinded saint. Later, others would name her

for a wild wife. Her mountains tinkle with springs
among moss-bearded forests, and the screeching of birds
stitches its tapestry. The white egret makes rings

stalking its pools. African fishermen make boards
from trees as tall as their gods with their echoing
axes, and a volcano, stinking with sulphur,

has made it a healing place." My voice was going
under the strength of his voice, which carried so far
that a black frigate heard it, steadying its wing.

I I

The charred ferryman kept rowing, black as the coal
on which the women climbed.
                              "Wha' happenin', bossman?"
He grinned, and I caught a dead whiff of alcohol;

but all islands have that legendary oarsman
slapping down dominoes on a rumshop table,
then raking the slabs in with a gravedigger's breath,

who grins and never loses. That comfortable,
common, familiar apparition of my death
spoke my own language, the one for which I had died,

his cracked soles braced against the rib of the gunwale,
not the marble tongue of the bust I sat beside,
and what was dying but the shadow of a sail

crossing this page or her face? That's why he had grinned,
rowing my ribbed trunk in sleep, it was he who steered
it to that other beach in an altering wind.

Now Seven Seas spoke to him, and the oarsman veered
the prow, braking an oar, and sculling it, until
the canoe was entering a hill-locked lagoon—

Marigot shot with fires of the immortelle,
with a crescent beach as thin as the quarter-moon,
virginal, inviolate, until the masts of war.

III

Seven Seas showed me the ghostly fleet at anchor
in that deep-draught shelter, assembled to destroy
their shadowy opposites, and spat in rancour

over the side of the pirogue. "This is like Troy
all over. This forest gathering for a face!
Only the years have changed since the weed-bearded kings.

Beyond these stone almonds I can see Comte de Grasse
pacing like horned Menelaus while his wife swings
her sandals by one hand, strutting a parapet,

knowing that her beauty is what no man can claim
any more than this bay. Her beauty stands apart
in a golden dress, its beaches wreathed with her name."

We rowed through the rotting fleet in a dead silence,
stirred only by the chuckle of the prow, then each mast
after reflection changed to a spindly fence

at the curve of a mangrove river, and then mist
blurred out Achille by his river. And then the bust
with its marble mouth revolved its irisless eyes.

Chapter LVIII

I

Up heights the Plunketts loved, from Soufrière upwards
past that ruined scheme which hawsers of lianas
had anchored in bush, of Messrs. Bennett & Ward,

the blind guide led me with a locked marble hand as
we smelt the foul sulphur of hell in paradise
on the brittle scab crusting its volcano's sores

and the scorching light that had put out Lucia's eyes
seared mine when I saw the Pool of Speculation
under its horned peaks. I heard the boiling engines

of steam in its fissures, the deep indignation
of Hephaestus or Ogun grumbling at the sins
of souls who had sold out their race, the ancient forge

of bubbling lead erupted with speculators
whose heads gurgled in the lava of the Malebolge
mumbling deals as they rose. These were the traitors

who, in elected office, saw the land as views
for hotels and elevated into waiters
the sons of others, while their own learnt something else.

Now, in their real estate, they lunged at my shoes
to pull me down with them as we walked along shelves
bubbling with secrets, with melting fingers of mud

and sucking faces that argued Necessity
in rapid zeroes which no one else understood
for the island's profit. One had rented the sea

to offshore trawlers, whose nets, if hoisted, would show
for thrice the length of its coast, while another thief
turned his black head like a ball in a casino

when the roulette wheel slowed down like his clicking teeth
in the pool's sluggish circle. It screamed in contempt
that choked in its bile at black people's laziness

whenever it leapt from the lava and then went
under again, then the shooting steam shot its price
from a fissure, as they went on making their deals

for the archipelago with hot, melting hands
before the price of their people dropped. The sandals
led me along the right path, around the fierce sands,

round the circle of speculation, where others
kept making room for slaves to betray their brothers,
till the eyes in the stone head were cursing their tears.

I I

Just as the nightingales had forgotten his lines,
cameras, not chimeras, saw his purple sea
as a postcard archipelago with gnarled pines

and godless temples, where the end of poetry
was a goat bleating down from the theatre steps
while the myrtles rustled like the dry sails of ships.

"You ain't been nowhere," Seven Seas said, "you have seen
nothing no matter how far you may have travelled,
cities with shadowy spires stitched on a screen

which the beak of a swift has ravelled and unravelled;
you have learnt no more than if you stood on that beach
watching the unthreading foam you watched as a youth,

except your skill with one oar; you hear the salt speech
that your father once heard; one island, and one truth.
Your wanderer is a phantom from the boy's shore.

Mark you, *he* does not go; he sends his narrator;
he plays tricks with time because there are two journeys
in every odyssey, one on worried water,

the other crouched and motionless, without noise.
For both, the 'I' is a mast; a desk is a raft
for one, foaming with paper, and dipping the beak

of a pen in its foam, while an actual craft
carries the other to cities where people speak
a different language, or look at him differently,

while the sun rises from the other direction
with its unsettling shadows, but the right journey
is motionless; as the sea moves round an island

that appears to be moving, love moves round the heart—
with encircling salt, and the slowly travelling hand
knows it returns to the port from which it must start.

Therefore, this is what this island has meant to you,
why my bust spoke, why the sea-swift was sent to you:
to circle yourself and your island with this art."

Helmets of mud-caked skulls. Out of the spectres
that the forge of the Malebolge was bubbling with,
a doubled shape stood up. Its grin was like Hector's.

Hector in hell, shouldering the lance of an oar!
In this place he had put himself in full belief
of an afterlife; a shadow in the geyser

that arched like a comet with its fountaining steam,
since for me not to have seen him there would question
a doctrine with more conviction than my own dream.

His charred face seemed to be travelling to the sun,
when its light broke through the changeable smoke once more,
since hell was certain to him as much as heaven;

now he was helmeted, and the borrowed visor
had slitted his face like an iguana's pods,
his shield a spiked hubcap, for the road-warrior

had paused in the smoke, not for Omeros's gods
nor the masks of his origins, the god-river,
the god-snake, but for the One that gathered his race

in the shoal of a net, a confirmed believer
in his own hell, that his spectre's punishment was
a halt in its passage towards a smokeless place.

There were Bennett & Ward! The two young Englishmen
in dirty pith-helmets crouched by the yellow sand
dribbling from the volcano's crust. Both were condemned

to pass a thermometer like that ampersand
which connected their names on a blackboard, its sign
coiled like a constrictor round the tree of Eden.

The stone heels guided me. I followed close behind
through the veils of stinking sulphur, filthy and frayed,
till I was as blind as it was, steering with one hand

in front of my face, beating webs from my forehead,
through the fool's gold of the yellow rocks, the thin sand
running from their fissures. But in such things, the guide

needs the trust of the wounded one to begin with;
he could feel my doubt behind him. That was no good.
I had lost faith both in religion and in myth.

In one pit were the poets. Selfish phantoms with eyes
who wrote with them only, saw only surfaces
in nature and men, and smiled at their similes,

condemned in their pit to weep at their own pages.
And that was where I had come from. Pride in my craft.
Elevating myself. I slid, and kept falling

towards the shit they stewed in; all the poets laughed,
jeering with dripping fingers; then Omeros gripped
my hand in enclosing marble and his strength moved

me away from that crowd, or else I might have slipped
to that backbiting circle, mockers and self-loved.
The blind feet guided me higher as the crust sloped.

As I, contemptuously, turned my head away,
a fist of ice gripped it from the soul-shaping forge,
and it wrenched my own head bubbling its half-lies,

crying out its name, but each noun stuck in its gorge
as it begged for pardon, willing to surrender
if another chance were given it at language.

But the ice-matted head hissed,
                              "You tried to render
their lives as you could, but that is never enough;
now in the sulphur's stench ask yourself this question,

whether a love of poverty helped you
to use other eyes, like those of that sightless stone?"
My own head sank in the black mud of Soufrière,

while it looked back with all the faith it could summon.
Both heads were turned like the god of the yawning year
on whose ridge I stood looking back where I came from.

The nightmare was gone. The bust became its own past,
I could still hear its white lines in the far-off foam.
I woke to hear blackbirds bickering at breakfast.

Chapter LIX

I

My light was clear. It defined the fallen schism
of a starfish, its asterisk printed on sand,
its homage to Omeros my exorcism.

I was an ant on the forehead of an atlas,
the stroke of one spidery palm on a cloud's page,
an asterisk only. Achille with his cutlass

rattling into the hold shared the same privilege
of an archipelago's dawn, a fresh language
salty and shared by the bittern's caw, by a frieze

of low pelicans. The sea was my privilege.
And a fresh people. The roar of famous cities
entered the sea-almond's branches and then tightened

into silence, and my crab's hand came out to write—
and down the January beach as it brightened
came bent sibyls sweeping the sand, then a hermit

waist-high in the empty bay, still splashing his face
in that immeasurable emptiness whose war
was between the clouds only. In that blessèd space

it was so quiet that I could hear the splutter
Philoctete made with his ablutions, and that deep "Ah!"
for the New Year's benediction. Then Philoctete

waved "Morning" to me from far, and I waved back;
we shared the one wound, the same cure. I felt the wet
sand under my soles, and the beach close like a book

behind me with every footmark. The morning's gift
was enough, but holier than that was the crab's lift-
ed pincer with its pen like the sea-dipping swift.

All the thunderous myths of that ocean were blown
up with the spray that dragged from the lacy bulwarks
of Cap's bracing headland. The sea had never known

any of them, nor had the illiterate rocks,
nor the circling frigates, nor even the white mesh
that knitted the Golden Fleece. The ocean had

no memory of the wanderings of Gilgamesh,
or whose sword severed whose head in the *Iliad*.
It was an epic where every line was erased

yet freshly written in sheets of exploding surf
in that blind violence with which one crest replaced
another with a trench and that heart-heaving sough

begun in Guinea to fountain exhaustion here,
however one read it, not as our defeat or
our victory; it drenched every survivor

with blessing. It never altered its metre
to suit the age, a wide page without metaphors.
Our last resort as much as yours, Omeros.

II

Why waste lines on Achille, a shade on the sea-floor?
Because strong as self-healing coral, a quiet culture
is branching from the white ribs of each ancestor,

deeper than it seems on the surface; slowly but sure,
it will change us with the fluent sculpture of Time,
it will grip like the polyp, soldered by the slime

of the sea-slug. Below him, a parodic architecture
re-erected the earth's crusted columns, its porous
temples, stoas through which whipping eels slide,

over him the tasselled palanquins of Portuguese man-o'-wars
bobbed like Asian potentates, when ribbed dunes hide
the spiked minarets, and the waving banners of moss

are the ghosts of motionless hordes. The crabs' anabasis
scuttles under his wake, because this is the true element,
water, which commemorates nothing in its stasis.

From that coral and crystalline origin, a simply decent
race broke from its various pasts, from howling sand
to a track in a forest, torn from the farthest places

of their nameless world. With nothing more in his hand
than the lance of a spear-gun, fishes keep shifting
direction like schools of philosophers,

and cautious plankton, who wait till darkness is lifting
from the Antillean seabed, burst into phosphorus,
meadows of stuttering praise. History has simplified

him. Its elegies had blinded me with the temporal
lament for a smoky Troy, but where coral died
it feeds on its death, the bones branch into more coral,

and contradiction begins. It lies in the schism
of the starfish reversing heaven; the mirror of History
has melted and, beneath it, a patient, hybrid organism

grows in his cruciform shadow. For a city
it had coral parthenons. No needling steeple
magnetized pilgrims, but it grew a good people.

God's light ripples over them as it does the Troumasse
River in the morning, as it does over me, when
the palm-wheel threshes its spokes, and my ecstasy

of privilege lifts me with the man-o'-war's wing
in that fear of happiness I have never shed,
pierced by a lance of sunlight flung over the sea.

O Sun, the one eye of heaven, O Force, O Light,
my heart kneels to you, my shadow has never changed
since the salt-fresh mornings of encircling delight

across whose cities the wings of the frigate ranged
freer than any republic, gliding with ancient
ease! I praise you not for my eyes. That other sight.

III

By the bay's cobalt, to that inaudible thud
that hits the forehead with its stunning width and hue,
the rage of Achille at being misunderstood

by a camera for the spelling on his canoe
was the same process by which men are simplified
as if they were horses, muscles made beautiful

by working the sea; by the deep clefts that divide
the plates of their chests, the iron wrists that can pull
a dead log up the wash alone, or, when the trench

of a breaker crests, how their soles turn into rocks,
though they are blurred for a while in the bursting drench
shifting a little for purchase. So an anchor

had hooked its rust in one sufferer, and the scar shows
on the slit bone still; so work was the prayer of anger
for a cursing Achille, who refused to strike a pose

for crouching photographers. So, if at the day's end
when they hauled with aching tendons the logged net,
their palms stinging dry with salt cuts from the stubborn seine,

the tourists came flying to them to capture the scene
like gulls fighting over a catch, Achille would howl
at their clacking cameras, and hurl an imagined lance!

It was the scream of a warrior losing his only soul
to the click of a Cyclops, the eye of its globing lens,
till they scuttered from his anger as a khaki mongrel

does from a kick. It was the last form of self-defence,
it was the scream of gangrene, and the vine round his heel
with its thorns. Waiters in bow-ties on the terrace

laughed at his anger. They too had been simplified.
They were like Lawrence crossing the sand with his trays.
They laughed at simplicities, the laugh of a wounded race.

Chapter LX

I

He had never seen such strange weather; the surprise
of a tempestuous January that churned
the foreshore brown with remarkable, bursting seas

convinced him that "somewhere people interfering
with the course of nature"; the feathery mare's tails
were more threateningly frequent, and its sunsets

the roaring ovens of the hurricane season,
while the frigates hung closer inland and the nets
starved on their bamboo poles. The rain lost its reason

and behaved with no sense at all. What had angered
the rain and made the sea foam? Seven Seas would talk
bewilderingly that man was an endangered

species now, a spectre, just like the Aruac
or the egret, or parrots screaming in terror
when men approached, and that once men were satisfied

with destroying men they would move on to Nature.
And those were the omens. He must not be afraid
once he kept his respect; the scarves of the sibyl

were those mare's tails over the island. Their changing
was beyond his strength and he was responsible
only to himself. The wisdom was enraging.

In fury, he sailed south, away from the trawlers
who were dredging the banks the way others had mined
the archipelago for silver. New silver was

the catch threshing the cavernous hold till each mound
was a pyramid; banks robbed by thirty-mile seines,
their refrigerated scales packed tightly as coins,

and no more lobsters on the seabed. All the signs
of a hidden devastation under the cones
of volcanic gorges. Every dawn made his trade

difficult and empty, sending him farther out
than he wanted to go, until he felt betrayed
by his calling, by a greed that had never banned

the voracious, insatiable nets. Fathoms where
he had seen the marlin buckle and leap were sand
clean at the bottom; the steely blue albacore

no longer leapt to his line, questioning dolphins,
yes, but the shrimp were finished, their bodies were curled
like exhausted Caribs in the deep silver mines;

was he the only fisherman left in the world
using the old ways, who believed his work was prayer,
who caught only enough, since the sea had to live,

because it was life? So he sailed down to Soufrière
along and close to the coast. He might have to leave
the village for good, its hotels and marinas,

the ice-packed shrimps of pink tourists, and find someplace,
some cove he could settle like another Aeneas,
founding not Rome but home, to survive in its peace,

far from the discos, the transports, the greed, the noise.
So he and Philoctete loaded the canoe and went
searching down the coastline, Anse La Raye, Canaries,

past cliffs pinned with birds, past beaches still innocent
where he saw a small boy alone, riding a log
and fishing with a twine, and the memory sent

a spear into his chest; he waved from the pirogue
but the small boy ignored him, just as Achille had
other boats long ago. Lean, supple, stark-naked.

But he found no cove he liked as much as his own
village, whatever the future brought, no inlet
spoke to him quietly, no bay parted its mouth

like Helen under him, so he told Philoctete
that until they found it they would keep going south,
as far as the Grenadines, though supplies were tight.

They spent the whole night on the beach in Soufrière,
talking to other fishermen under the horned,
holy peaks, where Achille built up a bonfire

to keep off the mosquitoes, where as the dry palms burned
he felt like the phantom of a vanishing race
of heroes, some toothless, some scarred, many of them turned

drunkards in the empty season, but in each face
by the cracking sparks there was that obvious wound
made from loving the sea over their own country.

Then he and Philoctete spoke till a hooked moon waned
and the twin horns sharpened out of a quiet sea.
They slept in the beached canoe till the sunlit wind

woke them and the other pirogues were setting out.
They washed and shat in the depot; they tried to find
a shop with some coffee, but all the doors were shut.

They saw what they thought were reefs wet with the morning
level light, seven miles nearer the Grenadines,
till they began passing the sail, and then a warning

cry from Philoctete, who was hauling in the lines
from the bow, showed him that the reefs were travelling
faster than they were, and begged him to shorten sail.

Exultant with terror, Philo kept ravelling
the line round his fist, and then both gasped as one whale—
"*Baleine*," said Achille—lifted its tapering wedge

as a bouquet of spume hissed from its splitting pod,
as it slowly heightened the island of itself,
then sounded, the tail sliding, till it disappeared

into a white hole whose trough, as it came, lifted
In God We Troust with its two men high off the shelf
of the open sea, then set it back down under

a swell that swamped them, while the indifferent shoal
foamed northward. He has seen the shut face of thunder,
he has known the frightening trough dividing the soul

from this life and the other, he has seen the pod
burst into spray. The bilge was bailed out, the sail
turned home, their wet, salted faces shining with God.

Chapter LXI

I

She was framed forever in the last century,
as was much of Ireland with its lace-draped parlours,
its shawled pianos, her antique maroon settee

(on auction after the Raj); it was not all hers,
this formal affection for candlelight on the
brass buttons of his Regimental mess-jacket,

those of an R.S.M., not a proper major,
since he loved it when she swirled her hair and packed it
in a bun spiked with a silver pin; when she wore

a frock with frothing collar and, like an oval
cameo, posed with one palm nesting the other
on the maroon couch with its parenthetical,

rhyming armrests—a daguerreotype of Mother—
which he studied as he wiggled one polished pump.
And sometimes she sang *a capella*, to the squeak

of his patent leather on the elephant stump
of the Indian hassock. It was so *fin de siècle*!
He often wondered if he'd fought the wrong war in

the wrong century. That swan-bowed, Victorian neck,
made whiter by its black-ribboned medallion,
would make him rise from his armchair and sail her hand

around the lances of the candles where Helen
waited in the shadows in that madras head-tie
that whitened her tolerant and enormous eyes.

It was all a lark. Like something out of Etty
or Alma-Tadema, those gold-framed memories,
stroking the tom in the dark with an ageing hand.

All her county shone in her face when the power
was cut, and the wick in the lamp would leap, as live
as the russet glints of her proud hair when she wore

it long and spread it over the wild grass to give
all that a girl could, with the camouflaged troop-ships
below them in the roadstead, with gulls buzzing the cliff

and screeching above us when she parted both lips
and searched for his soul with her tongue, her wild grey eyes
as flecked with light as the sea; then she was urging

me to go in, port of entry, with my fingers,
and I could not. Angry at being a virgin,
she turned her neck and I brushed the soft downy hair

from her ear's shelled perfection with archaic respect;
she steered my hand through the froth of her underwear,
sobbing, but with a firmness I didn't expect

from such a small wrist, but I couldn't. And then she
sat up and stared at the roots of the grass and smiled
faintly back at me. I said it was unlucky,

that I needed something to wait for, and perhaps
that was the nineteenth-century part, Tom. To be
more like an officer, and not one of those chaps

who knocked up beer-headed barmaids, got them with child,
and I told her that, stroking her huddled shoulders.
I wanted to believe in her more than the war;

it was like an old novel, with shawls and soldiers,
that's how it was, Tom. She said, "I feel like a whore,"
bending her white neck, stabbing her bun with a pin.

"Trying to trap you." I said, "We'll have a son, yes.
But this isn't the way you want this to happen
either." She took my fist and rubbed it with her tears.

They lay back on the grass, and after a while, her
tears stopped. He told her of an island he had seen
in an advert. An island where he could retire

if he lived through the war. She would give him a son.
Gnats were rising from the grass, and they watched the path
of the bent lances surrendering to the sun,

and the shining drops of the drizzle's aftermath
glittered like the letters by which she would be known
from that day forth, on that dragonfly afternoon.

The heat was hellish in the back of the rumshop.
The Major leant forward. The cane-bottom chair creaked.
Sweat clammed his khaki shirt. The sibyl closed her eyes

and removed her cracked lenses. The candle peaked
and the flame bent from one of those cavernous sighs
that came from the bowels of the earth. He waited.

She buried the sprig of croton to the brass bell's
tinkle in the open Bible, and he hated
the smell of fuming incense and everything else—

the lace doilies, the beads, his doubt.
                              "I see flat
water, like silver. I see your wife walking there
in a white dress with frills and pressing her white hat

with one hand in the breeze by a lake."
                              Glen-da-Lough.
But she could get that from any cheap calendar.
The Major smiled. She didn't have that far to look.

Close to Maud on the bed's shambles, he'd imagined
her soul as a small whirring thing that instantly
shot from its crumpled sheath, from its nest of dry vine,

to cross the tin roofs that furrowed into a sea
till, like a curlew lowering in the grey wind,
it saw the knolls and broken castles of Ireland.

Plunkett never thought he would ask the next question.
"Heaven?" He smiled.
                              "Yes. If heaven is a green place."
And her shut eyes watered while his own were open.

That moment bound him for good to another race.
Then the Major said, "Tell her something for me, please."
"She can hear you," the *gardeuse* said. "Just like in life."

"Tell her," said the Major, clearing his throat, "the keys . . .
that time when I slammed them, I'm sorry that I caused her
all that pain. Tell her"—he stopped—"that no other wife

would have borne so much." He lifted the small saucer
where the candle had shrunk to a stub, and he edged
a twenty-dollar bill under it, near the Bible.

I I

Ma Kilman opened her eyes, took her spectacles
off, and rubbed their cracked lenses. She was no sibyl
without them.
                              "She happy, sir." Like you oracles,

so would I be, he thought. A twenty-dollar bill
as an extra. He was rising from her table
of sweaty plastic when a white hand divided

the bamboo-bead curtain, and calm as Glen-da-Lough's
vision, Maud smiled, to let him through. The wound in his
head froze him in the scorched street. Innumerable flocks

of birds screamed from her guidebook over the shacks
of the village, their shadows like enormous fans,
all those she had sewn to the silken quilt, with tags

pinned to their spurs, and he knew her transparent hands
had unstitched them as he watched them flying over
the grooved roofs till they were simply the shadow of . . .

of a cloud on the hills. He sat in the Rover
and looked back at the No Pain Café. Maud closed the door
and sat next to him with the bread, beaming with love.

There was the same contentment in her demeanour
as when they had seen the old man with his grey bag
carrying the serpents' heads. He had not seen the

old labourer emerge from the unrolling flag
of smoke from his charcoal pit. The archangel showed
her how far he lived: in a cleft of green mountains

ridged like an iguana's spine. Under the old road
with its storm-echoing leaves, steady mountain winds
made the valley churn like wake at a liner's stern

and bent the green bamboos like archers; the old ones
creaking in their yellow joints. The track snaked through
ferns, wriggling up from the hidden river with the sign

S for serpent. He had turned his head away once;
but that was enough time for the apparition's
back to be sealed in bush, trembling at his return.

His wound healed slowly. He discovered the small joys
that lay in a life patterned like those on the quilt,
and he would speak to her in his normal voice

without feeling silly. Soon he lost any guilt
for her absence. Her absence was far, yet closer
than the blue hills of Saltibus in their cool light.

His memories opened the shutters of mimosa
like the lilies that widened in her pond at night
secretly, like angels, in the faith that was hers.

In the lion-clawed tub he idled in his bath,
he loved the nap of fresh towels, he scrubbed his ears
the way she insisted, he liked taking orders

from her invisible voice. He learned how to pause
in the shade of the stone arch watching the bright red
flowers of the immortelle, he forgot the war's

history that had cost him a son and wife. He read
calmly, and he began to speak to the workmen
not as boys who worked with him, till every name

somehow sounded different; when he thought of Helen
she was not a cause or a cloud, only a name
for a local wonder. He liked being alone

sometimes, and that was the best sign. He knew that Maud
was proud of him whenever the squared sunlight shone
on the taut comforter, that it was so well made.

Chapter LXII

Behind lace Christmas bush, the season's red sorrel,
what seemed a sunstruck stasis concealed a ferment
of lives behind tin fences, an endless quarrel

which Seven Seas recorded with no instrument
except ears sharper than his mongrel's; gardening
in his plot of old tires with violets, he'd hear them

over the roofs. He could hear the priest pardoning
their sins at vespers, the penitential anthem
of a Sunday in which no serious sins occurred.

The fishermen in black, rusty suits passed by him.
The helm of their turning week had come to a stop.
Seven Seas at his window heard their faint anthem:

"*Salve Regina*" in the pews of a stone ship,
which the black priest steered from his pulpit like a helm,
making the swift's sign from brow to muttering lip.

The village was surrendering a life besieged
by the lances of yachts in the white marina,
where egrets had hidden in the feathering reeds

of the lagoon. It had become a souvenir
of itself, and from the restaurant tables
with settings white as the yachts you could look towards

the marina's channel to the old weathered gables
of upstairs houses over the fishermen's yards
with biscuit-tin palings and cracked asphalt streets;

old tires wreathing a pier, vine-burdened fences,
an old woman pinning white, surrendering sheets
on a line. Its life adjusted to the lenses

of cameras that, perniciously elegiac,
took shots of passing things—Seven Seas and the dog
in the pharmacy's shade, every comic mistake

in spelling, like *In God We Troust* on a pirogue,
BLUE GENES, ARTLANTIC CITY, NO GABBAGE DUMPED HERE.
The village imitated the hotel brochure

with photogenic poverty, with atmosphere.
Those who were "people" lovers also have
a snapshot of Philoctete showing you his shin,

not saying how it was healed; some have Hector's grave
heaped with its shells, and an oar. All were welcomed in
the No Pain Café with its bamboo beads, then some

proceeded to the islet where a warped bottle
crusted with fool's gold in the amusing museum
shone like a false chalice, engravings of the Battle,

then a log with its entry, *Plunkett*, in lilac
ink. And, over and over again, the name Helen
of the West Indies, until they all turned their back

on the claim. They crushed the immortelle's vermilion
platoons under their sandals climbing to the redoubt,
from where they shot the humped island with its blue horns

and hazed Africa windward. None saw a swift dart
over the cactus on the cliff or heard it cry once.
Lizards emerged like tongues from the mouths of cannons.

I I

In the lion-coloured grass of the dry season
cannon gape at the sea from the windy summit,
their holes out of breath in the heat. If you rest one

palm on the hot iron barrel it will burn it,
but a lizard crawls there and raises its question:
"If this place is hers, did that empty horizon

once flash its broadsides with their inaudible rays
in her honour? Was that immense enterprise on
the baize tables of empires for one who carries

cheap sandals on a hooked finger with the Pitons
for breasts? Were both hemispheres the split breadfruit of
her African ass, her sea the fluted chitons

of a Greek frieze? And is she the Helen they love,
instead of a carved mouth with the almond's odour?
She walked on this parapet in a stolen dress,

she stood in a tilted shack with its open door.
Who gives her the palm? Did sulking Achille grapple
with Hector to repeat themselves? Exchange a spear

for a cutlass; and when Paris tosses the apple
from his palm to Venus, make it a *pomme-Cythère*,
make all those parallels pointless. Names are not oars

312

that have to be laid side by side, nor are legends;
slowly the foaming clouds have forgotten ours.
You were never in Troy, and, between two Helens,

yours is here and alive; their classic features
were turned into silhouettes from the lightning bolt
of a glance. These Helens are different creatures,

one marble, one ebony. One unknots a belt
of yellow cotton slowly from her shelving waist,
one a cord of purple wool, the other one takes

a bracelet of white cowries from a narrow wrist;
one lies in a room with olive-eyed mosaics,
another in a beach shack with its straw mattress,

but each draws an elbow slowly over her face
and offers the gift of her sculptured nakedness,
parting her mouth. The sanderlings lift with their cries.

And those birds Maud Plunkett stitched into her green silk
with sibylline steadiness were what islands bred:
brown dove, black grackle, herons like ewers of milk,

pinned to a habitat many had adopted.
The lakes of the world have their own diaspora
of birds every winter, but these would not return.

The African swallow, the finch from India
now spoke the white language of a tea-sipping tern,
with the Chinese nightingales on a shantung screen,

while the Persian falcon, whose cry leaves a scar
on the sky till it closes, saw the sand turn green,
the dunes to sea, understudying the man-o'-war,

talking the marine dialect of the Caribbean
with nightjars, finches, and swallows, each origin
enriching the islands to which their cries were sewn.

Across the bay the ridge bristled once with a fort,
then the inner promontory itself; its shipping
was martial then, its traffic in masts the swift fleet

of both navies; sails soared to the boatswain's piping,
like Seven Seas's kettle, squadrons would slowly surge
from volcanic inlets. Its map, riddled with bays

like an almond leaf, provided defence or siege,
but its cannons, set in their spiked circle, could blaze
like the forehead of Mars. Now French, now British yards

fluttered from its mornes; no sooner was one flag set
than another battle unravelled its lanyards
and a bugle hoisted the other. Each sunset,

with its charred flagships, its smouldering fires, its coals
fanned by the breeze at landfall, dilated and died,
every Redcoat an ember, its garrisoned souls

shouldering their muskets like palm-fronds until Parade
marched into night's black oblivion that vizored
Mars' brow. Along the horizon in a green flash

a headland swallowed the sun's leaf like a lizard
to the thudding cannonballs of a calabash.
Then long shadows alternated like the keyboard

of Plunkett's piano to the fringed lamp of the moon,
as the siege and battles were changed to its shawled song
crossing the sea. Now there were hundreds of Frenchmen

and British listening in their separate cemeteries,
who died for a lizard, for red leaves to belong
to their ranks, for that green flash that was History's.

III

Galleons of clouds are becalmed, waiting for a wind.
The lizard spins on its tripod, panning, to find
the boulders below where slaves built the breakwater.

The Battle of the Saints moves through the surf of trees.
School-texts rustle to the oval portrait of a
cloud-wigged Rodney, but the builders' names are not there,

not Hector's ancestor's, Philoctete's, nor Achille's.
The blue sky is a French tunic, its Croix de Guerre
the sunburst of a medal. The engraved ovals

of both admirals fit, when a schoolbook closes,
into one locket. Screaming only in vowels,
the children burst out of History. Some classes

race past the breakwater, the anonymous cairn
carried by a line of black ants, some up the street
to crouch under the window-ledge by Ma Kilman,

to shout at his elbow and frighten Philoctete,
then yell: "Aye! Seven Seas!" in their American
accent. One stalks near the growling dog on a bet.

Their books are closed like the folded wings of a moth.
The lizard leaps into the grass. You bend your head
to hear "Iounalo" from the cannon's mouth.

Chapter LXIII

Seven Seas sat anchored in the rumshop window,
the khaki dog stretched at his feet clicking at flies.
The Saturday sunlight laid a map on the floor

and smaller maps on his shades. Hefting the empties
from the blocko, the girl took them out the back door
to stack them near the gate. She was Ma Kilman's niece

fresh from the country, and the village was for her
a startling city, its music widening her eyes
like a new Helen. The dog's tail thudded the floor.

The hot deck of the rumshop idled like a ship
becalmed in Saturday's doldrums. In the rocker
Ma Kilman yawned, steering them into deep gossip.

"Statics is her uncle, the girl. He went Florida,
after the election, as a migrant-picker.
You know Maljo. Didier? That man worried her,

yes, with his outside children plus what he stick her
with, but this one, my godchild, is legitimate.
She very obedient. She will make a good maid."

"I know Florida," Seven Seas said. "The life better
there, but not good. That is the trouble with the States."
"Statics change," she said. "Somebody bring a letter

316

home from him. Christine, you go and sit by those crates
in the yard and call me when the sweet-drink truck come."
The girl went out to the yard.
                              "A long letter home.

His job is to put the oranges in a sack
one by one, as if they is islands."
                              "In the South,"
Seven Seas said, "the Deep South, you musn't talk back.

You do what the white man give you and shut your mouth."
"Anyway," she sighed, "Statics meet this Cherokee
woman, a wild Indian, you know, and they live well

together. 'Good electricity,' he say. He
send her photo to his wife, so his wife could tell
people she know a real Indian, not a West

Indian. I see the picture and she look real wild,
not with feathers and so on, but with big, big breast
like she ready! Which is why I send out the child.

Aye, aye! Statics send to say one night at a bar,
a true-true Indian come in and next thing he know
this Choctaw truck-driver lift him by the collar

and start choking him, and he tell the woman, 'Let's blow,
babe,' and leave Statics high and dry like a canoe.
Statics write to say his woman now is the dollar."

Helen came into the shop, and she had that slow
feline smile of a pregnant woman, the slow grace
that can go with it. Sometimes the gods will hallow

all of a race's beauty in a single face.
She wanted some margarine. Ma Kilman showed her where
the tubs were kept in the freezer. Helen chose one,

then she paid Ma Kilman and left. The dividing air
closed in her wake, and the shop went into shadow,
with the map on the floor, as if she were the sun.

"She making child," she said. "Achille want to give it,
even is Hector's, an African name. Helen
don't want no African child. He say he'll leave it

till the day of the christening. That Helen must learn
where she from. Philo standing godfather. You see?
Standing, Philo, standing straight! That sore used to burn

that man till he bawl, *songez?*"
                                        "I heard his agony
from the yam garden," Seven Seas said. "They doing well,
the white yams. The sea-breeze does season them with salt."

He hummed in the silence. The song of the chanterelle,
the river griot, the Sioux shaman. Asphalt
rippled its wires, like a harp. The street was still.

Seven Seas sighed. What was the original fault?
"Plunkett promise me a pig next Christmas. He'll heal
in time, too."
       "We shall all heal."
               The incurable

wound of time pierced them down the long, sharp-shadowed street.
A thudding wave. The sunlight setting a table.
And the distant drone of a comet. The sibyl

snored. Seven Seas sat there as if carved in marble.
His beard white, his hands on the cane, very still.
A swift squeaked like a hinge, then shot from the windowsill.

III

I followed a sea-swift to both sides of this text;
her hyphen stitched its seam, like the interlocking
basins of a globe in which one half fits the next

into an equator, both shores neatly clicking
into a globe; except that its meridian
was not North and South but East and West. One, the New

World, made exactly like the Old, halves of one brain,
or the beat of both hands rowing that bear the two
vessels of the heart with balance, weight, and design.

Her wing-beat carries these islands to Africa,
she sewed the Atlantic rift with a needle's line,
the rift in the soul. Now, as vision grows weaker,

319

it glimpses the straightened X of the soaring swift,
like a cedar's branches widening in sunrise,
in oars that are crossed and settled in calm water,

since the place held all I needed of paradise,
with no other sign but a lizard's signature,
and no other laurel but the *laurier-cannelle's.*

Chapter LXIV

I

I sang of quiet Achille, Afolabe's son,
who never ascended in an elevator,
who had no passport, since the horizon needs none,

never begged nor borrowed, was nobody's waiter,
whose end, when it comes, will be a death by water
(which is not for this book, which will remain unknown

and unread by him). I sang the only slaughter
that brought him delight, and that from necessity—
of fish, sang the channels of his back in the sun.

I sang our wide country, the Caribbean Sea.
Who hated shoes, whose soles were as cracked as a stone,
who was gentle with ropes, who had one suit alone,

whom no man dared insult and who insulted no one,
whose grin was a white breaker cresting, but whose frown
was a growing thunderhead, whose fist of iron

would do me a greater honour if it held on
to my casket's oarlocks than mine lifting his own
when both anchors are lowered in the one island,

but now the idyll dies, the goblet is broken,
and rainwater trickles down the brown cheek of a jar
from the clay of Choiseul. So much left unspoken

by my chirping nib! And my earth-door lies ajar.
I lie wrapped in a flour-sack sail. The clods thud
on my rope-lowered canoe. Rasping shovels scrape

a dry rain of dirt on its hold, but turn your head
when the sea-almond rattles or the rust-leaved grape
from the shells of my unpharaonic pyramid

towards paper shredded by the wind and scattered
like white gulls that separate their names from the foam
and nod to a fisherman with his khaki dog

that skitters from the wave-crash, then frown at his form
for one swift second. In its earth-trough, my pirogue
with its brass-handled oarlocks is sailing. Not from

but with them, with Hector, with Maud in the rhythm
of her beds trowelled over, with a swirling log
lifting its mossed head from the swell; let the deep hymn

of the Caribbean continue my epilogue;
may waves remove their shawls as my mourners walk home
to their rusted villages, good shoes in one hand,

passing a boy who walked through the ignorant foam,
and saw a sail going out or else coming in,
and watched asterisks of rain puckering the sand.

You can see Helen at the Halcyon. She is dressed
in the national costume: white, low-cut bodice,
with frilled lace at the collar, just a cleft of a breast

for the customers when she places their orders
on the shields of the tables. They can guess the rest
under the madras skirt with its golden borders

and the flirtatious knot of the madras head-tie.
She pauses between the tables, holding a tray
over her stomach to hide the wave-rounded sigh

of her pregnancy. There is something too remote
about her stillness. Women study her beauty,
but turn their faces away if their eyes should meet,

like an ebony carving. But if she should swerve
that silhouette hammered out of the sea's metal
like a profile on a shield, its sinuous neck

longing like a palm's, you might recall that battle
for which they named an island or the heaving wreck
of the *Ville de Paris* in her foam-frilled bodice,

or just think, "What a fine local woman!" and her
head will turn when you snap your fingers, the slow eyes
approaching you with the leisure of a panther

through white tables with palm-green iron umbrellas,
past children wading with water-wings in the pool;
and Africa strides, not alabaster Hellas,

and half the world lies open to show its black pearl.
She waits for your order and you lower your eyes
away from hers that have never carried the spoil

of Troy, that never betrayed horned Menelaus
or netted Agamemnon in their irises.
But the name Helen had gripped my wrist in its vise

to plunge it into the foaming page. For three years,
phantom hearer, I kept wandering to a voice
hoarse as winter's echo in the throat of a vase!

Like Philoctete's wound, this language carries its cure,
its radiant affliction; reluctantly now,
like Achille's, my craft slips the chain of its anchor,

moored to its cross as I leave it; its nodding prow
lettered as simply, ribbed in our native timber,
riding these last worried lines; its rhythm agrees

that all it forgot a swift made it remember
since that green sunrise of axes and laurel-trees,
till the sunset chars it, slowly, to an ember.

And Achille himself had been one of those children
whose voices are surf under a galvanized roof;
sheep bleating in the schoolyard; a Caribbean

whose woolly crests were the backs of the Cyclops's flock,
with the smart man under one's belly. Blue stories
we recited as children lifted with the rock

of Polyphemus. From a plaster Omeros
the smoke and the scarves of mare's tails, continually
chalked associate phantoms across our own sky.

Out of their element, the thrashing mackerel
thudded, silver, then leaden. The vermilion scales
of snappers faded like sunset. The wet, mossed coral

sea-fans that winnowed weeds in the wiry water
stiffened to bony lace, and the dripping tendrils
of an octopus wrung its hands at the slaughter

from the gutting knives. Achille unstitched the entrails
and hurled them on the sand for the palm-ribbed mongrels
and the sawing flies. As skittish as hyenas

the dogs trotted, then paused, angling their muzzles
sideways to gnaw on trembling legs, then lift a nose
at more scavengers. A triumphant Achilles,

his hands gloved in blood, moved to the other canoes
whose hulls were thumping with fishes. In the spread seine
the silvery mackerel multiplied the noise

of coins in a basin. The copper scales, swaying,
were balanced by one iron tear; then there was peace.
They washed their short knives, they wrapped the flour-bag sails,

then they helped him haul *In God We Troust* back in place,
jamming logs under its keel. He felt his muscles
unknotting like rope. The nets were closing their eyes,

sagging on bamboo poles near the concrete depot.
In the standpipe's sandy trough aching Achilles
washed sand from his heels, then tightened the brass spigot

to its last drop. An immense lilac emptiness
settled the sea. He sniffed his name in one armpit.
He scraped dry scales off his hands. He liked the odours

of the sea in him. Night was fanning its coalpot
from one catching star. The No Pain lit its doors
in the village. Achille put the wedge of dolphin

that he'd saved for Helen in Hector's rusty tin.
A full moon shone like a slice of raw onion.
When he left the beach the sea was still going on.